Salad Days

RECIPES FOR DELICIOUS, ORGANIC SALADS AND DRESSINGS FOR EVERY SEASON

PAM POWELL
The Salad Girl

Voyageur Press

Spring Salads

Summer Salads

Autumn Salads

Winter Salads

Introduction

MY SALAD DAYS BEGAN when I was a teenager, working as a dishwasher at Madden's Pine Beach Lodge & Resort in Brainerd, Minnesota, during the summer. From a busy kitchen, in a restaurant in a part of the resort called Lumber Town U.S.A., came family-style Minnesota walleye and farmhouse-baked chicken dinners with all the fixings.

I was busy, but during my breaks between lunch and dinner I was able to assist the kitchen's "salad girl" with her chores: preparing all the fresh vegetables for the relish trays, peeling and crinkle-cutting the carrots, peeling potatoes for mashing, and preparing greens for the salads and cabbage for the homemade slaw. I found that I had a real knack for fresh food preparation and I really loved eating the raw, fresh vegetables that were being delivered directly from the local farms. Then, the happy day came when I was promoted from dishwasher to "salad girl." This was the beginning of a lifetime passion for preparing fresh, unique, and creative salads.

I learned every part of the food industry at Madden's—from dishwashing and food prep to waitressing and bartending. With these skills in my apron pocket, I was able to get a job at any restaurant to help put myself through art school. It wasn't until the late 1970s, when I got a job at a hip little vegetarian restaurant called Café Kardamena, that I understood the important link between eating well and good health. Café Kardamena, located in the historic Summit Hill area of St. Paul, was owned by Brenda Langton, a beautiful, twenty-something visionary who was dedicated to spreading the good news about the importance of eating right by sharing flavorful whole-foods dishes with her customers. Brenda combined fresh, raw foods and simple, real ingredients to achieve amazing flavor combinations. Brenda was also one of the first local female chefs to create lasting and mutually beneficial relationships with the local farmers and fisheries that supplied food to her restaurant.

Working with Brenda shaped my belief that cooking and eating organic whole foods that are produced without the use of synthetic fertilizers, artificial pesticides, herbicides, antibiotics, growth hormones, feed additives, or genetically modified organisms not only makes us healthy and happy, but it also keeps our planet healthy.

After art school, I became a freelance artist with a full-time job as a private chef in a household in White Bear Lake, Minnesota. Our son, Nick, was just a toddler, and my husband, Jim, was almost done with college when we decided to start a little weekend catering business for extra money. My favorite part of planning the catering menus was designing a recipe for an organic, seasonal salad. At times, I would design the whole menu around the salad! My clients loved my organic salad dressings so much that they started to special-order them to give to family and friends as gifts throughout the year.

In spring 2006, the owner of Kowalski's Markets, a local grocery store chain, tasted my dressings and invited me to put them on the refrigerated shelves of all eight of the company's stores. This meant that I needed to increase the volume of my manufacturing capacity to meet the demands of produce department orders, obtain organic certification for each flavor, and create a safe shelf life without impacting the fresh flavors of the dressings. I like a challenge, and this was a once-in-a-lifetime opportunity for me to make a dream come true, so with a lot of support, love, and elbow grease from my family and friends, I decided to take the leap of faith, and that spring, Salad Girl Inc. was born. We began to sell our unique salad dressings made with all organic ingredients at the Mill City Farmers' Market (founded by Brenda Langton, chef/owner of Café Kardamena, Café Brenda, and Spoonriver Restaurant), located next to the famous Guthrie Theater on the banks of the Mississippi River in Minneapolis.

Every week we worked in the evenings after our day jobs to bottle about 100 bottles of Salad Girl Organic Dressings, and each weekend we sold them all at the market. Our maximum bottling capacity was about 200 bottles, and we could never make enough to satisfy demand. Soon we outgrew the two commercial kitchens we had rented and were blessed to find a certified organic co-packing facility in Cannon Falls, Minnesota. These folks were so kind to lend our little local company a helping hand, and because of their help, we were able to make enough dressing to fill our first big order for Kowalski's in March 2007.

We put our first four varieties of certified organic Fresh Dressings for Fresh Greens on the refrigerated shelves of the eight stores by Easter. We started with our farmers' market bestsellers: Crisp Apple Maple, Curry and Fig, Pomegranate Pear, and Blueberry Basil. Now, three years later, Salad Girl Inc. creates and manufactures six fresh garden-inspired flavors of certified organic salad dressings that can be found on the refrigerated shelves of the produce department in many Whole Foods Markets, specialty food markets, co-ops, and

natural foods stores throughout the country. (Go to www.saladgirl.com or http://thesaladgirlsblog.com for more information on where to find Salad Girl Organic Dressings.)

Throughout the book, you will find that I have used artisan cheeses crafted in the United States and sustainable U.S. seafoods. The websites for these ingredients are listed in the Resources section at the end of the book. I have also included a number of tips that focus on shopping for and keeping fresh sustainable salad ingredients. I hope you find these ideas for healthier eating and a healthier environment helpful.

I am so happy to be able to share my recipes with you. I hope that as you craft these seasonal, artisan salads for your family and friends, you will feel the health, happiness, and joy I have experienced by creating them!

Greens 101

A SALAD IS ONLY AS GOOD as the ingredients used to create it. Start by selecting greens that are packed with flavor. Fresh, organic dark leafy greens, such as the varieties described here, have more nutritional value per forkful than lighter-colored varieties like iceberg.

ARUGULA: Arugula, pronounced ah-ROO-guh-lah, is one of the first greens of spring. It has a very distinctive flavor of spicy pepper with a hint of nut. Arugula is a good source of antioxidants, vitamins A and C, potassium, and calcium. The leaves should be bright green and fresh looking. Arugula is also called rocket, roquette, rugula, and ruccola *(also called garden rocket, rocket salad, Italian cress, Mediterranean rocket, wild rocket)*.

BABY BEET GREENS: The leafy greens of immature beets are edible, tasty, and very nutritious *(also known as baby beet tops, beet tops, beet)*.

BUTTERHEAD LETTUCE: Succulent and sweet, butterhead lettuces have soft, pale green to yellow-green leaves that are small and round. The best-known varieties of butterhead lettuces include Bibb and Boston lettuce *(also called butter lettuce)*.

CRESS: Cress is appreciated for its sharp flavor and attractive appearance for garnishes. Two major types of cresses include upland cress and watercress. **Watercress**, a popular member of the mustard family, has delicate, small, bright green leaves that provide a peppery, tangy flavor. It is a good source of potassium and iron. **Upland cress** is similar in appearance to its better-known cousin, watercress. It is a member of the mustard family and packs a sharp, peppery flavor. Upland cress is also known by several other names, including American cress, land cress, winter cress, cassabully, and creasy salad, and it boasts a deeper pungency than watercress. Other varieties of cress include peppergrass *(also called curly cress)*, garden cress, and broadleaf cress.

DANDELION GREENS: Dandelions are actually a member of the sunflower family. They will be the tastiest in early spring before the flowers emerge, so purchase or harvest the dandelion greens when the leaves are small and young.

ENDIVE: Endive is available in three varieties. **Belgian endive**, interestingly, is grown in total darkness to prevent the leaves from greening. It is also know as French endive and has tightly bundled, slightly bitter, white-cream leaves with yellow-green tips. **Curly endive** has green, lacy

Arugula

Baby Beet Greens

Baby Bib

Cress

leaves that curl at the tips (*also known as frisée, chicory, chicory endive, curly chicory*). **Escarole** has a milder flavor and broad, pale green leaves (*also known as Batavian endive, Bavarian endive, grumolo, scarole, broad-leaved endive*).

FRISÉE: Frisée, a member of the chicory family, has curly, fringed, narrow leaves and a mildly bitter taste. The white, delicate center has a less bitter taste than the outer leaves.

KALE: Kale is actually a member of the cabbage family. It is attractive with a bold flavor that can be slightly bitter (*also called curly kale, ornamental kale, Georgia collards, dinosaur kale, salad savoy*).

LOOSE LEAF LETTUCE: Green leaf, red leaf, and oak leaf are the most popular leaf lettuce varieties (*also called leaf lettuce, bunching lettuce*). **Red leaf** lettuce, with reddish-bronze frilly leaves, has a mild flavor offering folate and vitamin A. **Green leaf** lettuce varies in color from medium to dark green with darker leaves providing more vitamin A. They provide a crisp texture and mild flavor. **Oak leaf** lettuce, named for its oak-shaped leaves, is a decorative, tender, and very flavorful lettuce.

MÂCHE: The dark green, narrow leaves of this very special variety of lettuce known as mâche are tender with a unique slightly sweet, tangy, nutlike flavor. Mâche is a good source of vitamin A and beta carotene (*also known as lamb's lettuce, Rapunzel, field salad, corn salad, Lewiston corn salad, field lettuce*).

MIZUNA: Mizuna is an Asian specialty vegetable nicknamed "spider mustard." It has jagged-edged, narrow leaves that have a peppery, nutty flavor similar to arugula (*also known as Japanese greens, Oriental greens, xiu cai, kyona, potherb mustard, and California peppergrass*).

MUSTARD GREENS: Mustard greens, with their frilled edges, dark green leaves, and bold, pungent flavor, should be used quickly after purchase, as they are very perishable (*also called leaf mustard, Indian mustard, mustard, brown mustard*).

RADDICHIO: Radicchio, pronounced rahd-EEK-ee-o, resembles a small head of cabbage with very attractive dark burgundy, shiny leaves and contrasting white ribs and a distinctive bittersweet taste (*also called Chioggia, red chicory, red leaf chicory, red Italian chicory*).

ROMAINE: Dark green outer leaves that pale toward the center, romaine leaves are crispy and slightly bitter but flavorful. Romaine has a long, narrow head with a very tasty midrib (*also called cos, cos lettuce, little gem lettuce, lattuga romana, laitue romaine, bindesalat, römischer salat, sommerendivie, lechuga romana, alface romana*).

SPINACH: An excellent source of antioxidants including beta carotene, spinach is extremely versatile, attractive with its dark green foliage, and delicious.

TANGO: Tango lettuce has frilly leaves and looks quite a bit like endive. It has a mild, tangy taste. Tango lettuce is full of vitamins and easy to grow.

TATSOI: Tasting similar to spinach but milder, tatsoi is a dark green Asian salad green with a flat, rosette shape. Its individual leaves are spoon-shaped with a sweet aroma (*also known as tat soi or tot soi, spoon cabbage, spinach mustard, flat back cabbage, rosette bok choy, pak choy, Chinese flat cabbage*).

TURNIP GREENS: The leaves of turnips are slightly sweet when young but strong-flavored and tough with age. Turnip greens are a great source of vitamin A and vitamin C (*also called turnip tops, turnip leaves*).

Escarole

Dandelion Greens

WASHING YOUR PRODUCE

Some nifty and sustainable tools for storing freshly washed greens, fresh fruits, and vegetables are now available in the marketplace. Crate and Barrel (www.crateandbarrel.com) stocks some of the best and most affordable sustainable food containers. Whether produce is organically grown or conventionally grown, it is really important to wash your leafy greens, fruits, and vegetables thoroughly and properly.

To wash your produce, follow these simple steps:

1. Start by keeping your kitchen countertops, refrigerator, cookware, and cutlery clean. Make a bottle of a safe, natural wash right in your own kitchen to help clean your fresh produce, kitchen countertops, etc. (see the recipe below in number 7).

2. Always wash your hands before preparing meals and handling fruits and vegetables.

3. Keep fresh greens, fruits, and vegetables away from uncooked meats to avoid cross-contamination.

4. Choose healthy-looking, ripe fruits and vegetables when you shop. Avoid bruised, moldy, and mushy produce.

5. Wait until just before you eat or prepare your fruits and vegetables to wash them. Fruits and vegetables have natural coatings that keep moisture inside, and washing them will make them spoil sooner.

6. Wash all parts of your fruits and vegetables, even if you don't plan on eating them. Bacteria can live on the rind of an orange or the skin of a cucumber, for example. Though you may peel them away and toss them in the trash, the bacteria can be transferred from the outside of the fruit or vegetable to the knife you use to cut them and then onto the parts you will be eating.

7. Don't use any soaps, detergents, bleaches, or other toxic cleaning chemicals when cleaning fresh produce. These just leave another chemical residue behind. Instead, make a bottle of safe, natural veggie wash to help clean your fresh produce. In a new, unused and empty 1-qt. spray bottle, mix together the following: 3 tbsp. organic lemon juice, 2 tbsp. baking soda, 1 c. fresh filtered water, and ¾ c. white vinegar. Shake well before each use.

8. Spray firmer fruits and vegetables, such as apples and potatoes, with produce wash, let sit 2–3 minutes, and immerse in tub of cold water. Scrub with a vegetable brush while rinsing with clean water to remove dirt and residues.

9. Rinse berries and other small fruits thoroughly and allow them to drain in a colander.

10. **Washing lettuces and leafy greens:** Thoroughly clean both sides of a double kitchen sink and fill one side full of cold, clean water. Add 1½ c. of the fresh produce wash. Lay two clean cotton towels out on the kitchen counter to drain and dry fresh greens. Remove and discard the outer leaves of lettuce, and immerse the remaining leaves in cold water, carefully swishing each leaf one at a time in the cool water. Place in a clean colander in the second sink, and when colander is full, rinse the greens again in the second sink with fresh water. Place each leaf on a clean, dry double kitchen cotton towel to dry and drain, then place in a salad spinner for a gentle spin. I use the extra water from the salad spinner to water my flower box herbs.

    Store delicate fresh greens longer by wrapping clean greens loosely in a clean, dry flour sack towel and then in a bio-degradable airtight cellulose bag available at www.greenhome.com. Before sealing the bag, gently squeeze out as much air as possible without squashing greens.

A WELL-STOCKED SALAD-MAKING KITCHEN

The secret to a great salad is quality ingredients. I suggest you stock your pantry with the following items to make your salads extra-special. Keep in mind that quality ingredients can be expensive, so we recommend adding one or two of these extra pantry items to your shopping list at a time. Keep one or two of the fresh items on hand at a time. Fresh citrus, fresh herbs, or garlic are good choices. I've included a list of my favorite oils and vinegars in the Resources section at the back of the book.

OILS: To make the best homemade salad dressing, choose good-quality oil. Many food markets carry a wonderful assortment of naturally processed, cold-pressed, and expeller-pressed oils. Many of these are perfect for salads, such as avocado oil, organic sunflower oil, walnut oil, and pumpkin seed oil. All of these oils are full of wonderful nutrients and antioxidants and create a unique flavor note when used in different salad dressing recipes. Roasted nut oils, such as walnut or hazelnut (incredibly delicate and delicious), sweeten and toast the flavor of dressings. Using olive oils from different regions where the flavor of the oil depends on the climate, region, growing method, and the olive itself will add another dimension to the flavor profile of the dressings you create. The flavor of olive oil can be strong, peppery, spicy, grassy, or even mellow and mild. There is a myriad of unique flavor combinations with which to be creative.

VINEGARS: Vinegars and citrus juices add acidity, which provides a nice balance in flavor and gives your salad some "pep." Fortunately, we live in a time where many food markets carry a wonderful assortment of vinegars with a wide range of flavors. Read your labels for ingredients in the vinegar, and be aware of where your ingredients are coming from and where the vinegar is processed. When you open a bottle, taste the vinegar. It will be sharp, yes, but you should enjoy its flavor, not cringe from it. If vinegar is not your thing, there are plenty of other options, such as citrus fruit juice. A good ratio of oil to vinegar is about 3:1, but this depends on your personal taste. Here are some of your vinegar options.

- Rice vinegar
- Chardonnay white wine vinegar (or other white wine vinegar)
- Balsamic vinegar—darker and a little sweeter
- Raw, unpasteurized apple cider vinegar—delivers live enzymes and probiotics
- Red wine vinegar—very tangy and acidic
- Sherry vinegar—more subtle flavor than red wine vinegar
- Flavored vinegars (basil, garlic, thyme, lemongrass)
- Citrus fruit juices (orange, grapefruit, blood oranges, lemon, lime)
- Fruit juices (pomegranate, apple, cranberry, blueberry, cherry)

FRESH LEMONS, LIMES, ORANGES, GRAPEFRUITS: These can be used as the "acid" in a salad dressing, replacing the vinegar.

MUSTARD: Mustard is an important ingredient used to emulsify, creating a thicker oil and vinegar dressing. There is an abundant selection of fancy mustards available to experiment with on the food market shelves today. Some of my favorite mustards are made by SoNo Mustards, based in San Diego, California. SoNo sells seven great flavors of mustard that really make a dressing or vinaigrette pop.

WHOLE FRUIT SYRUPS: Fruit preserves are a great addition to vinaigrettes and dressings. Most store-bought preserves, even the organic ones, are made with cane sugar and pectin. If you would rather avoid cane sugar, make your own. I've included my daughter-in-law's recipe for whole fruit syrup made with a bit of honey, agave, or maple syrup on page 13.

FRESH OR DRIED HERBS: Creating fresh salads and salad dressings is the number one reason to plant a few herbs in pots on the patio, balcony, or kitchen. Good choices are chives, French tarragon, basil, thyme, oregano, and cilantro. If you're purchasing your fresh herbs, buy one bunch or packet at a time from the supermarket to experiment with as you like. Be careful, as they are quite perishable.

FRESH GARLIC, SWEET ONIONS, SHALLOTS, GREEN ONIONS (SCALLIONS): Wonders for many salads and salad dressing recipes.

MILK AND CREAM: Low-fat buttermilk, cream, and milk are common ingredients in creamy salad dressings.

CHEESE: Local artisan cheeses are the perfect complement to crunchy fresh greens, fruits, and vegetables. We have chosen some really unique, delicious, and award-winning artisan cheeses sourced from all over the United States in our salad recipes. You can find these cheeses in the Resources section in the back of the book.

SALAD SUNDRIES: A variety of organic olives, sun-dried tomatoes, hearts of palm, marinated artichokes, and roasted red peppers are great to have available.

DRIED NUTS AND SEEDS: The toasty, buttery crunch of nuts and seeds can make the ordinary salad extraordinary. Stock up on an assortment of these tasty nuts and seeds: pecans, almonds, pistachio kernels, walnuts, cashews, hazelnuts, pine nuts, sunflower seeds, sesame seeds, and pumpkin seeds (pepitas). For the best flavor, roast your own, following the instructions on page 13.

DRIED GRAINS: Keep an assortment of the following on hand: bulgur, quinoa (black, red, and plain), wild rice, couscous, and brown rice.

SUSTAINABLE PROTEINS: Adding meat, poultry, or fish to your salad creates a healthy main dish meal in minutes! Use our Resources section for assistance in purchasing safe and sustainable proteins.

BASIC RECIPES

SIMPLE VINAIGRETTE

To make simple, perfect vinaigrettes, begin with three basic ingredients: a healthy fat, an acid, and, if you want a "creamy" dressing, an emulsifier. Here is an easy recipe that takes less than 5 minutes to prepare. You will need a sturdy glass mixing bowl, wire whisk, measuring cup, and tablespoon.

Add 2 tbsp. of acid (balsamic vinegar, rice vinegar, orange or lemon juice—see Vinegars on page 11 and Fresh Lemons, Limes, Oranges, Grapefruits above for other ideas) to a medium bowl.

Next, whisk in a tablespoon of Dijon mustard. This acts as an emulsifying agent, which binds the oil and vinegar together.

Next is the addition of 1 c. of a healthy fat. To achieve the best taste and texture, it's important to choose a good, freshly bottled local organic salad oil (see Oils and Vinegars on page 11).

The addition of the oil to the mustard and acid mixture is the key chemical ingredient to a smooth emulsified vinaigrette. You will need two hands for making truly successful vinaigrettes: one hand to whisk the ingredients together while the other pours in the oil. Use a damp flour sack cloth beneath your bowl to keep it from sliding and then add the oil in a slow, steady stream while whisking continuously and vigorously until everything is incorporated well and emulsified. If you've got a blender, use it. I have a handy little Rocket Blender by Bella Cucina Artful Food (www. bellacucina.com) that comes with different-sized glass containers with covers for easy storage.

Get creative. Don't be afraid to improvise. You will find this basic recipe perfect for adding your own unique touch to your salads. The salad recipes in this book follow this same simple process.

Order of operation is important. Remember to add all ingredients to the emulsifier and acid mixture before slowly pouring in the oil. Season to taste with salt and pepper, and your vinaigrette is done and ready for the tasting.

ANNA'S ORGANIC HONEY AND WHOLE FRUIT CONCENTRATE   MAKES 16 OZ.

This whole fruit syrup is excellent to use in salad dressing. You also can use the concentrate for flavored iced teas, lemonade, and healthy frozen treats.

Bring 4 c. washed organic fruit (blueberries, raspberries, strawberries, currants, rhubarb, cherries, pomegranate seeds, nectarines, peaches, plums) and ½ c. organic, local honey (¼ c. agave syrup) to a gentle boil. Turn down to lowest simmer, and stir occasionally and carefully with a potato masher to macerate the fruit gently. Simmer fruit on lowest heat, and thicken for about 1 hour. Remove from heat, and if very pulpy or full of skin, strain through sieve. Cool and store in a wide-mouthed glass jar. Cover and refrigerate. This will be good to use for 2–3 weeks.

ROASTED NUTS

Low and slow is the key to successful roasting. Here's how to roast nuts perfectly every time.

Preheat oven to 275°F. Place 1 c. nuts in mixing bowl. Add ½ tsp. olive oil (omit if you prefer dry-roasted nuts) and ⅛ tsp. sea salt. Toss together, and spread out on shallow baking pan. Roast for length of time below, until nuts are fragrant and lightly browned. Crumble into fine, sandlike crumbs, and set aside for later use.

- If you are roasting walnuts, you may use walnut oil here instead.

- Roast pine nuts for 15–20 minutes; pecans and walnuts for 20–30 minutes; hazelnuts for 40–50 minutes; pistachios, almonds, sunflower seeds, and cashews for 30–40 minutes.

Spring Salads

I KNOW IT IS TRULY SPRING when my chives begin to stretch their bright green blades toward the sky, forecasting the preparation of a spring Quinoa Tabbouleh. And the greens! Watercress, mâche, beet greens, arugula, pea shoots, and the first tiny bunching onions appear, begging for our attention. Rhubarb is not far behind, with its brilliant red stalks, tart and sweet, virtually demanding to be made into a Strawberry-Rhubarb Vinaigrette.

In the spring, the more adventuresome foodies forgo their market baskets for hiking boots and can be found wandering the countryside in search of wild ramps, fiddlehead ferns, wild asparagus, and morels. These same spring delights are sold at local farmers' markets for the short time they are in season. Whether you gather these delicious, fresh spring flavors from your own garden, from a walk in the woods, or from the local farmers' market, savor spring by crafting beautiful artisan salads to share with family and friends.

Spring Marinated Asparagus Salad with Simple Spring Vinaigrette

THE FIRST SIGHT OF svelte, green perennial bundles of asparagus at the local markets heralds the beginning of spring. Asparagus, a member of the lily family, was once known as "sparrow grass." Fresh asparagus of all colors—green, purple, or white—provides an earthy, sweet aperitif to the main course of summer's bounty. Serve this salad on a large platter or in a shallow salad bowl.

2 lb. spring asparagus

5 oz. heirloom lettuces, washed and dried
(baby oak leaf, baby Boston red, little gem)

1 c. Solé GranQueso cheese, finely shredded
(If Solé GranQueso is not available, ask your cheesemonger for a similar tasting local cheese.)

1 c. green pistachios, roasted (see recipe on page 13)

1: **PREPARE THE VINAIGRETTE.**

2: **PREPARE ASPARAGUS.** The tender tips of asparagus can be especially sandy. Wash the asparagus by holding the bunch upside down. Gently swish in cold water. Then, to snap off the tough woody bottoms, bend the stalk at the natural breaking point (where the color changes from white to green, 1–2 in. from the base). Cook the asparagus al dente (still crispy and green). Place cooled asparagus in shallow glass dish, and cover with half of the Simple Spring Vinaigrette. Marinate in refrigerator for 1 hour.

3: **ASSEMBLE SALAD.** Arrange heirloom greens upon a pretty platter, decorate with nicely stacked bundles of marinated asparagus, and sprinkle with the cheese and pistachios. Just before serving, drizzle the Simple Spring Vinaigrette over the salad. Serve remaining vinaigrette in a little pitcher on the side.

Simple Spring Vinaigrette

4 tbsp. clover honey
8 tbsp. rice vinegar
2 tsp. Dijon mustard
2 tsp. sea salt
1 tsp. ground black pepper
1 c. olive oil

Pour honey, rice vinegar, mustard, salt, and ground pepper into a small blender, and blend together just to combine. Add in the olive oil, and blend until emulsified (binding vinegar and olive oil together). Pour into a little glass jar, cover, and keep cool until ready to serve salad. Shake it up to recombine ingredients before drizzling on the salads. Use half for the marinade and half for the assembled salad.

Buy Local: Asparagus

In the spring, your local farmers' markets will have delicious asparagus available. Buying local produce that is in season and organic is the greenest way to go. Get to know your farmers at the market. To find a farmers' market near you, check out www.localharvest.org.

Sautéed Fiddlehead Fern and Mâche Salad with Spring Ramp Vinaigrette

FIDDLEHEAD FERNS ARE THE NEW, springtime growth of the ostrich fern and are named because the coiled shoots look like a little fiddle. They taste of green beans with a hint of artichoke—a unique flavor of their own. Other types of fern shoots can be toxic, so fiddleheads should always be bought from a reputable produce seller. Fiddlehead ferns are only available for a few weeks in the spring, so enjoy this salad while you can!

5 oz. spring mâche

16 freshly picked fiddlehead ferns (from a reputable produce market)

2 tsp. coarse salt

Juice of ½ fresh lemon

2–3 tbsp. olive oil

Fresh-ground pepper

½ c. SarVecchio Parmesan cheese, grated (If SarVecchio is not available, ask your cheesemonger for a parmesan-style local cheese.)

1: PREPARE THE VINAIGRETTE.

2: PREPARE FERNS. To clean the ferns, remove the dry, sheathlike papery particles and any brown skin from the fiddleheads. Fill a medium bowl with cool water. Add 1 tsp. salt and the lemon juice. Add ferns, and push them down into the water several times to clean them. Transfer to cotton towel to drain. Place a steamer rack over 1 in. of water in a saucepan. Steam the fiddleheads, covered, for 4–5 minutes, until tender. Heat olive oil in a large skillet over medium heat. Add fiddleheads, and cook 1–2 minutes on each side, until golden. Season with salt and pepper, and set aside.

3: ASSEMBLE SALAD. Divide mâche that has been washed and dried among 6–8 salad plates. Divide and arrange the sautéed fiddleheads on greens, and adorn with a nice ribbon of the grated cheese. Serve right away with Spring Ramp Vinaigrette drizzled over the salad.

Spring Ramp Vinaigrette

1 bunch ramps
1 c. olive oil
2 tbsp. balsamic vinegar

1 tsp. brown sugar
Coarse sea salt and ground pepper

Wash ramps and pat dry. Remove the stringy roots, and separate the larger white bulbs from the ramps. Roughly chop the stems and leaves. Heat the olive oil in a sauté pan over medium heat and add bulbs. Sauté until tender and just beginning to brown. Add remaining ramp stems and leaves, and cook until wilted. Turn heat down to low, and add the vinegar and brown sugar. Whisk in the rest of the olive oil, and remove from heat while still whisking. Salt and pepper to taste. Spoon some of the ramp bulbs and pieces of the leaves upon each fiddlehead salad along with the warm vinaigrette.

Arugula and Asparagus Salad with Zesty Lemon Vinaigrette

ARUGULA IS ONE OF THE FIRST greens of spring. It has a very distinctive flavor of spicy pepper with a hint of nut. Arugula is a good source of antioxidants, vitamins A and C, potassium, and calcium. In this salad, the flavors of the arugula, asparagus, and lemon blend together perfectly.

1½ lb. fresh asparagus

2 c. spring peas

5 oz. fresh baby arugula

1½ c. Ladysmith cheese, grated large
   (Similar to an Italian ricotta salata)

½ c. roasted hazelnuts (see page 13)

1 tbsp. lemon zest strips (thin julienned strips of lemon rind)

1: **PREPARE THE VINAIGRETTE.**

2: **PREPARE ASPARAGUS.** The tender tips of asparagus can be especially sandy. Holding bunch upside down, gently swish in cold water. Then, to snap off the tough woody bottoms, bend the stalk at the natural breaking point, about 1–2 in. from the base. To blanch, bring 2 c. water to boil in a shallow pan, add the asparagus, and turn off the burner. After 4–5 minutes, drain, and rinse with cold water to stop the cooking process. They should be bright green and tender crisp. Set aside.

3: **PREPARE OTHER PRODUCE.** Begin by washing the pea pods thoroughly to remove any dirt and grit. Snap off both ends of the pea pod. Remove the strip in the middle and pry open the pod at the seam using your thumbs. Rake the peas out of the pod using your fingers, and let them drop into the empty container. Wash and dry the baby arugula.

4: **ASSEMBLE SALAD.** Arrange arugula (divided on plates or arranged on large platter). Sprinkle with cheese, decorate with fresh peas and asparagus, and sprinkle with nuts and julienned lemon zest. Just before serving, drizzle with Zesty Lemon Vinaigrette.

Zesty Lemon Vinaigrette

4 tbsp. fresh organic
   Meyer lemon juice

2 tbsp. honey

2 tsp. Dijon mustard

1 tsp. sea salt

½ tsp. ground black
   pepper

½ c. olive oil

Pour lemon juice, honey, mustard, salt, and ground pepper into a small blender. Blend ingredients together to completely combine. Pour into a bowl, and slowly whisk in the olive oil until thoroughly combined. Pour into a glass jar, cover, and keep cool until ready to assemble salad. Shake it up to recombine ingredients before drizzling on salads.

Ravishing Radish Salad
with Chive and Cracked Pepper Vinaigrette

THIS SALAD IS BEST when made using a variety of radishes. Two "show-stopper" winter radishes, which are available in spring, are the Watermelon and Black Spanish varieties. Try to include some of these radishes when you prepare this recipe, if they are available. Their unusual shapes and beautiful colors make great food for fodder at any spring gathering!

16 spring radishes (Choose at least 4 varieties, using half of each radish per salad.)

5 oz. baby spinach leaves

2 c. stringless sugar snap peas

4 oz. chèvre cheese, crumbled (If you choose a log or cake of chèvre, freeze it until it is firm and then crumble it.)

1 c. roasted hazelnuts (see page 13)

1: PREPARE THE VINAIGRETTE.

2: PREPARE RADISHES. Choose four of each of the varieties of radishes. Wrap the rest of the radishes in a dry, clean flour sack towel and refrigerate. Trim off stems, roots, and green leaves of radishes and wash. Let drain and dry. Slice the oval radishes into thin, round slices. Slice the longer radishes into matchstick diagonals. If you have successfully acquired the "watermelon" variety of radish, cut this in thin round slices and then cut like a pie into little wedges. Wrap prepped radishes in a damp flour sack towel and put into the refrigerator until you're ready to assemble the salad.

3: PREPARE OTHER PRODUCE. Wash and dry baby spinach leaves. Wash and dry sugar snap peas, then cut into halves diagonally.

4: ASSEMBLE SALAD. This salad may be plated by dividing the spinach greens among eight salad plates. Sprinkle first with the chèvre and then the hazelnuts, fan the watermelon radishes, and scatter sugar snap peas and round sliced radishes in and upon the greens. Stack together the matchstick-cut radishes, and just before serving, drizzle with the Chive and Cracked Pepper Vinaigrette.

Chive and Cracked Pepper Vinaigrette

4 tbsp. rice vinegar

1 tbsp. honey

½ tbsp. Dijon mustard

2 tbsp. fresh chives, chopped

1 tsp. sea salt

½ tsp. ground black pepper

½ c. olive oil

Put vinegar, honey, mustard, finely minced chives, salt, and ground pepper into a small blender. Blend ingredients together to completely combine. Pour into a bowl, and slowly whisk in the olive oil until thoroughly combined. Pour into a glass jar, cover, and keep cool until ready to assemble salad. Shake it up to recombine ingredients before drizzling on salads.

Fresh Fig and Mesclun Salad with Sweet Honey Vinaigrette

THIS SALAD FEATURES fresh Brown Turkey figs, which taste like a combination of strawberry and peach and are golden yellow when ripe. Fresh figs are a good source of iron, calcium, vitamin B6, and protein.

8 fresh Brown Turkey figs

5 oz. fresh spring mesclun, washed and dried

8 oz. Uplands Pleasant Ridge cheese, grated (If Uplands Pleasant Ridge is not available, ask your cheesemonger for a similar tasting local cheese.)

1 c. roasted walnuts (see recipe on page 13)

1: **PREPARE THE VINAIGRETTE.**

2: **PREPARE FIGS.** For an attractive presentation, without cutting through the stem, make a crisscross cut on the bottom of the fig, allowing the fruit to fan open.

3: **ASSEMBLE SALAD.** Garnish 8 salad plates with the mesclun, and place a fig on each. Place 1 oz. of grated cheese alongside the fig, and sprinkle with walnuts. Just before serving, drizzle with the Sweet Honey Vinaigrette.

Sweet Honey Vinaigrette

4 tbsp. balsamic vinegar
5 tbsp. honey
1 tbsp. Dijon mustard
1 tbsp. Vidalia onion, chopped
1 tsp. sea salt
½ tsp. ground black pepper
½ c. olive oil

Pour vinegar, honey, mustard, Vidalia onion, salt, and ground pepper into a small blender. Blend ingredients together to completely combine. Pour into a bowl, and slowly whisk in the olive oil until thoroughly combined. Pour into a glass jar, cover, and keep cool until ready to assemble salad. Shake it up to recombine ingredients before drizzling on salads.

Keep It Fresh

Fresh figs are very perishable and should be kept refrigerated. The recommended storage temperature for figs is 32–36°F. To store, place on a paper towel, cover with plastic, and refrigerate up to 3 days. Use ripe figs immediately. Fresh figs will store for as long as 5–7 days. Figs may be frozen in a sealed bag or a sealed container for up to 6 months.

Mother's Day Melon and Baby Spring Greens Salad with Cilantro Lime Vinaigrette

THIS REFRESHING SALAD uses a combination of orange and green muskmelons. When selecting muskmelons, look for those that give off a sweet odor and are slightly soft at the blossom end of the fruit. Directions here are for plated salads, but this refreshing, nutritious salad can be served on a platter as well.

½ Golden Kiss melon, cantaloupe, or other sweet orange melon, cold

½ honeydew or other sweet green melon, cold

2 avocados

5 oz. mixed baby spring greens, washed

4 oz. Shepherds Way Friesago (a semi-hard sheep milk cheese with a piquant, slightly nutty flavor)

Cracked pepper

1 c. roasted walnuts (see recipe on page 13)

¼ tsp. zest of lime

Fresh cilantro sprig for decoration

1: **PREPARE THE VINAIGRETTE.**

2: **PREPARE MELONS.** Wash the melons, then cut in half and remove seeds. Cut each melon into quarters and then into eighths, then into sixteenths. Remove the skin from the melon and cut each of the segments into 4 thin slices. Place all the slices in neat stacks of 4 on a clean, dry towel on a cookie sheet. Cover and put in refrigerator until ready to use.

3: **PREPARE AVOCADOS.** Grip the avocado gently on one side with your hand. With a sharp paring knife, cut the avocado lengthwise around the seed, then use both hands to twist two halves counterclockwise just enough to free half from pit. Open the two halves to expose the pit, then cut into quarters, and gently remove each quarter from the pit. Peel off the skin from each quarter, and slice each quarter into 4 slices.

4: **PLATE THE SALADS.** Divide and mound greens onto 8 pretty spring plates, fan melon and avocado slices alternating slice of orange melon, slice of avocado, slice of honey dew, slice of avocado. Cut a ½ in. by 1 in. wedge of cheese, and place on the bottom of the fanned fruit. Sprinkle salads with walnuts and cracked pepper, and decorate with zest of lime and a sprig of cilantro. Pass the Cilantro Lime Vinaigrette in a pretty little pitcher.

Cilantro Lime Vinaigrette

2 tbsp. honey

¼ c. fresh lime juice

⅛ leftover section of lime, rind and meat

1 tbsp. fresh cilantro

1 tbsp. sweet onion

1 tsp. sea salt

1 tsp. ground black pepper

½ c. walnut oil (organic, if available)

Pour honey, lime juice, piece of lime, cilantro, onion, salt, and ground pepper into a small blender. Blend ingredients together until smooth. Place mixture into a bowl, and whisk in the walnut oil. **NOTE:** you can add the walnut oil to the blender and blend all ingredients together until smooth and blended well, but don't overdo it, as it can get too thick in the blender. Pour vinaigrette into a small glass jar, cover, and keep cool until ready to serve salad.

Pea Sprout and Strawberry Salad
with Strawberry Rhubarb Vinaigrette

FRESH PEA SPROUTS, the young leaves and tendrils of sweet sugar snap pea vines or snow pea vines, or from any other type of edible garden pea, are available at your local farmers' market or in your garden in spring and early summer. These pretty, winding, leafy greens have a fresh, crisp, clean pea flavor and are the perfect little greens to add to your spring salads.

1 lb. strawberries, organic

5 oz. spring arugula

2 c. tops of fresh pea sprouts

1 c. new green peas, shelled

1½ c. Hidden Springs Farmstead Feta Cheese, crumbled (or a comparable local feta cheese)

1 c. roasted almonds (see recipe on page 13)

1: **PREPARE THE VINAIGRETTE.**

2: **PREPARE STRAWBERRIES.** Gently wash and dry. Pick out 5 beautiful berries and set aside. Hull or snip off all of the stems of the other strawberries, and cut into fourths. Set aside in a cool place.

3: **PREPARE PRODUCE.** Wash and dry the spring arugula, pea sprouts, and shelled new green peas.

4: **ASSEMBLE SALAD.** Arrange half the arugula on a platter. Sprinkle with half the feta, half the shelled peas, half the quartered strawberries, and half the pea sprouts. Add rest of arugula and feta. Add the crumbled almonds and the rest of the peas, quartered strawberries, and pea sprouts. Cut the reserved stemmed strawberries in half and arrange them gently among the pea sprouts. Keep it cool. Just before serving, drizzle with Strawberry Rhubarb Vinaigrette.

Strawberry Rhubarb Vinaigrette

½ c. light and buttery-flavored olive oil

¼ c. rice vinegar

⅓ c. fresh rhubarb, chopped

3 tbsp. strawberry preserves

2 tbsp. sweet Vidalia onion, minced

1 tsp. sea salt

1 tsp. finely ground black pepper

Place all vinaigrette ingredients into a small blender. Blend together just until smooth and completely blended (about 10 seconds). Don't blend it too long, as it will get too thick. Pour the vinaigrette into a small glass jar, cover, and refrigerate until ready to use. **NOTE:** Do not eat or compost rhubarb leaves. They are poisonous.

Baby New Potato and Upland Cress Salad with Chive and Cracked Pepper Vinaigrette

CRESS, A MEMBER OF the mustard family, packs a sharp, peppery flavor. The upland cress used in this salad is similar in appearance to its better-known cousin, watercress, and is a great of source vitamin C, potassium, and iron.

12 small baby new potatoes

3 oz. upland cress

6 oz. chèvre cheese, crumbled (If you choose a log or cake of chèvre, freeze it until it is firm and then crumble it. Choose Stickney Hill Chèvre made in Minnesota, Painted Goat Chèvre made in New York, or another chèvre goat cheese if made closer to your home.)

1: **PREPARE THE VINAIGRETTE.**

2: **PREPARE BABY NEW POTATOES.** Use a vegetable brush to clean. Cut into halves. Cover potatoes with water and bring water to a boil. Simmer on low for 10 minutes. Check with a knife to see if potatoes are done. Rinse with cool water, drain, and cool.

3: **PREPARE UPLAND CRESS.** Remove the stems and wash. Dry cress, and cut chiffonade style (thin strips).

4: **ASSEMBLE SALAD.** Gently combine potatoes, upland cress, chèvre, and Chive and Cracked Pepper Vinaigrette in a large bowl. Toss carefully so as not to mash the potatoes but to thoroughly coat them with cheese. Place in the refrigerator until ready to serve. This can be prepared hours before mealtime.

Chive and Cracked Pepper Vinaigrette

4 tbsp. rice vinegar
1 tbsp. honey
1 tbsp. stone-ground mustard
2 tbsp. fresh chives, minced

1 tsp. sea salt
½ tsp. ground black pepper
½ c. olive oil

Put vinegar, honey, mustard, finely minced chives, salt, and ground pepper into a small blender. Blend ingredients together to completely combine. Pour into a bowl, and slowly whisk in the olive oil until thoroughly combined. Pour into a glass jar, cover, and keep cool until ready to assemble salad. Just before serving, shake it up before drizzling on salads.

Curried Hen Salad
with Creamy Curry and Honey Dressing

SERVES 6–8

THE CRUNCHY CASHEWS, juicy grapes, crisp apples, Curry and Honey Dressing, and wonderful texture of the dried Zante currants make this salad like no other salad you've ever experienced. Bon appétit!

5 chicken breasts
5 oz. spinach leaves
½ c. fresh green grapes
½ c. fresh red grapes
2 c. tart orchard apple
½ c. scallions
½ c. dried Zante currants
1½ c. roasted cashews (reserve 2 tbsp. for decoration) (see recipe on page 13)

1: **PREPARE THE DRESSING.**

2: **GRILL CHICKEN BREAST.** To preheat the grill before cooking, set all burners on high heat, and close the lid. Heat for 10 minutes or until thermometer registers 500–550°F. Turn down to medium heat, and with the lid down, cook chicken 6½ minutes per side or until the meat thermometer reads 160°F. Let the chicken cool, and cut into ¼-in. chunks. Keep refrigerated until ready to assemble salad.

3: **PREPARE PRODUCE.** Wash and dry all produce. Cut spinach chiffonade, cut grapes in halves, and chop apples and scallions.

4: **COMBINE** chicken, apples, Zante currants, cashews, onion, and grapes with the Creamy Curry and Honey Dressing, folding in gently, combining all the ingredients with the dressing.

5: **ASSEMBLE SALADS.** Divide and arrange spinach chiffonade like little nests on 6–8 salad plates or little teacups. Scoop mound of the curried chicken salad onto each, and sprinkle with cashews.

Creamy Curry and Honey Dressing

1 tbsp. red onion, minced
¼ c. rice vinegar
¼ c. olive oil
2 tbsp. honey
1 tsp. sea salt
½ tsp. ground black pepper

½ tbsp. curry powder (Use this amount first, taste, and then add more curry if desired.)
1½ c. olive oil–based mayonnaise

Put first 7 dressing ingredients into blender and whirl until combined and smooth. Pour into deep 2-qt. glass bowl, and gently whisk with mayonnaise. Keep cool until ready to use.

Grilled Pork Tenderloin Medallions on Spring Greens with Rosemary and Rhubarb Vinaigrette

IT WOULDN'T BE SPRING without savoring the taste of some garden-grown rhubarb. This is a hearty salad with great contrasting flavors!

4 lb. pork tenderloin

7 oz. mixed spring greens

8 sprigs fresh rosemary

8 spring green onions

1 pink stalk rhubarb without leaves

1 c. SarVecchio Parmesan cheese, large grated
(or a comparable local, parmesan-style cheese)

1 c. roasted pecans (see recipe on page 13)

1: **PREPARE THE VINAIGRETTE.**

2: **PREPARE PORK.** Place the pork tenderloins in a bowl with reserved vinaigrette, making sure to cover all the meat with the Rosemary and Rhubarb Vinaigrette. Marinate for 1 hour in the refrigerator. To preheat the grill, set all grill burners on high heat, and close the lid. Heat for 10 minutes or until thermometer registers 500–550°F. Sear the pork on direct high heat for 2–4 minutes per side, then turn grill down to medium, and with the lid down, grill tenderloin for 5–6 minutes per side or until meat thermometer reads 155°F for "medium" (slightly pink inside for perfectly grilled pork). Let the meat cool, and cut into ½-in. medallions. Keep refrigerated until ready to assemble salad.

3: **PREPARE PRODUCE.** Wash and dry spring greens, rosemary sprigs, 6-in. stalk of fresh rhubarb, and green onions. Zest the rhubarb in long, curly ribbons. Cut roots off of onions and slice each onion in half the long way from the white bulb on the bottom to green top. Set aside.

4: **ASSEMBLE SALAD.** Divide and arrange spring greens on dinner plates, sprinkle with grated cheese, arrange 2–3 medallions of pork on the greens, place onions on the side of greens, and decorate with sprigs of rosemary and rhubarb ribbon. Sprinkle with roasted nuts, and, just before serving, drizzle Rosemary and Rhubarb Vinaigrette over each salad.

Rosemary and Rhubarb Vinaigrette

8 tbsp. balsamic vinegar

6 tbsp. honey

1 tbsp. Dijon mustard

1 c. rhubarb, chopped

1 green onion

1 tsp. fresh rosemary

2 tsp. sea salt

1 tsp. ground black pepper

1 c. extra-virgin olive oil

Put balsamic vinegar, honey, mustard, rhubarb, onion, rosemary, sea salt, and pepper into a small blender. Blend ingredients together until smooth, and pour into a glass bowl. Slowly whisk in the oil (be careful not to whisk too much) until smooth and emulsified. Put half the vinaigrette in a bowl for the pork marinade. Pour the rest into a small glass jar. Cover and keep cool until ready to serve salad.

Red Raspberries and Spring Mâche Salad with Raspberry and Pink Peppercorn Vinaigrette

THE DARK GREEN, narrow leaves of the very special variety of lettuce known as mâche are tender with a unique, slightly sweet, tangy, nutlike flavor. Mâche is a good source of vitamin A and beta carotene. Mâche absorbs moisture and loses its texture with time, so it is best to wait until the last minute before putting the vinaigrette on this exquisite spring salad.

8 slices of grainy and seedy honey whole-wheat bread

2 tbsp. butter, softened

4 oz. fresh Bent River Camembert-style cheese (If Bent River is not available, ask your cheesemonger for a similar tasting local cheese.)

5 oz. fresh spring mâche

4 white salad turnips

1 pt. fresh raspberries

½ c. roasted hazelnuts (see recipe on page 13)

1: **PREPARE THE VINAIGRETTE.**

2: **PREPARE CROUTONS.** Using a cookie or crouton cutter, cut 8–10 croutons from the whole-wheat and seeded bread. Brush with ⅛ tsp. butter, and toast in the oven on a cookie sheet for 12 minutes at 275°F until crispy. Set aside and cool. Cut 16 little squares of the camembert cheese with a sharp knife. After the croutons have cooled, place cheese on each crouton, and sprinkle with a half turn of the pink peppercorn grinder. Set aside.

3: **PREPARE PRODUCE.** Wash and dry the mâche and turnips. Cut the turnips baton (matchsticks). Very gently wash and dry the raspberries right before assembly of the salad.

4: **ASSEMBLE SALADS.** Divide mâche among 6–8 salad plates, sprinkle with turnip matchsticks, place crouton on top of the mâche in the center, and decorate with berries in a circle around the crouton. Sprinkle with crumbled hazelnuts, and, just before serving, drizzle with Raspberry and Pink Peppercorn Vinaigrette.

Raspberry and Pink Peppercorn Vinaigrette

¼ c. balsamic vinegar

3 tbsp. raspberry preserves

1 tsp. stone-ground mustard

1 tsp. sea salt

½ tsp. pink peppercorns

½ c. fruity olive oil

Put balsamic vinegar, raspberry preserves, stone-ground mustard, sea salt, and pink peppercorns into a small blender. Blend just to combine. Pour into a glass bowl and slowly whisk in the olive oil. The mixture should be smooth and emulsified. Pour it into a small glass jar, cover, and keep cool until ready to serve salad.

Spring Bing Cherry and Curly Cress Salad with Ginger Cherry Vinaigrette

SERVES 6–8

THE COMBINATION OF cherry and ginger flavors in this salad is amazing. Bing cherries—large, deliciously sweet cherries with a deep-red/garnet color—are a good source of antioxidants.

3 c. fresh bing cherries

5 oz. garden green leaf lettuce

1–2 oz. curly cress (with blossoms if available for decoration)

2 c. fresh sugar snap peas

6–8 slices red onion

1 c. San Andreas farmstead cheese, grated (If San Andreas cheese is not available, ask your cheesemonger for a comparable local, Pecorino-style cheese.)

½ c. roasted cashews (see recipe on page 13)

1: **PREPARE THE VINAIGRETTE.**

2: **PREPARE CHERRIES.** Wash cherries, and remove stems on all cherries except one or two for décor. Cut in halves, and remove pits. Set aside, and keep cool.

3: **PREPARE OTHER PRODUCE.** Wash and dry the garden green leaf lettuce and curly cress. Wash and dry the sugar snap peas, and then cut in halves diagonally. Cut the red onion into thin slices.

4: **ASSEMBLE SALAD.** Arrange half the greens on a pretty platter, decorate with half the cress, half the cheese, half the nuts, half the onions, half the sugar snap peas, half the cherries, and then repeat. Decorate with some of the curly cress blossoms. Just before serving, drizzle with Ginger Cherry Vinaigrette.

Ginger Cherry Vinaigrette

¼ c. rice vinegar

3 tbsp. cherry preserves (see page 13 for cherry whole fruit syrup)

1 tbsp. fresh ginger, skin removed

½ clove fresh shallot or

fresh garlic

⅛ tsp. sesame oil

1 tsp. sea salt

½ tsp. black pepper

½ c. olive oil

Place vinegar, cherry preserves, ginger, shallot/garlic, sesame oil, sea salt, and pepper into a small blender. Blend ingredients together until smooth, and then pour these ingredients into a glass bowl. Slowly whisk in the olive oil (be careful not to whisk too much) until smooth and emulsified. Pour the vinaigrette into a small glass jar, and set aside in a cool place until ready to use.

Buy Organic

Buy organic cherries whenever possible, as the fruit ranks ninth on the list of produce with the highest pesticide loads. If you enjoy picking your own cherries, check for a local grower that meets your standards, www.pickyourown.org.

Asparagus Caesar with
Creamy SarVecchio Parmesan Caesar Dressing

THE RICH, NUTTY taste of SarVecchio Parmesan gives this salad a unique and delicious flavor. If SarVecchio is not available, look for a comparable local parmesan cheese.

1 baguette

½ c. extra-virgin olive oil

½ tsp. dried basil

½ tsp. dried oregano

1 c. SarVecchio Parmesan cheese, finely grated
(or a comparable local parmesan cheese)

2 lb. spring asparagus tips

1 sweet red pepper

7 oz. romaine lettuce leaves

1: PREPARE THE DRESSING.

2: PREPARE CROUTONS. Preheat oven to 250°F, cut baguette into 1/4-in. squares, put squares in big glass bowl, and toss with ½ c. extra-virgin olive oil, dried basil, dried oregano, and grated cheese. Spread out on a cookie sheet and toast for 20–25 minutes, until golden and crunchy. Let cool and set aside.

3: PREPARE ASPARAGUS AND RED PEPPER. The tender tips of asparagus can be especially sandy. Wash the asparagus by holding bunch upside down. Gently swish in cold water. Then, to snap off the tough woody bottoms, bend the stalk at the natural breaking point (where the color changes from white to green, 1–2 in. from the base). Cook the asparagus al dente (still crispy and green). Cut the tips and stems into 3-in. pieces. Wash the red pepper and cut into 3-in. julienned strips. Set aside.

4: PREPARE ROMAINE LEAVES. Wash, dry, and chop into large, uniform, bite-sized pieces with lettuce knife. Set aside.

5: ASSEMBLE SALAD. In a big wooden salad bowl, combine romaine, red pepper strips, and asparagus. Pour on Creamy SarVecchio Parmesan Caesar Dressing, toss together, and sprinkle with the croutons and the rest of the dressing. Serve immediately.

Creamy SarVecchio Parmesan Caesar Dressing

4 tbsp. lemon juice

2 tbsp. honey

1 tbsp. fresh basil

½ clove garlic

1 tsp. sea salt

1 tsp. black pepper

1½ c. olive oil–based mayonnaise

2 tbsp. extra-virgin olive oil

½ c. SarVecchio Parmesan cheese, finely grated (or comparable local parmesan cheese)

Put lemon juice, honey, fresh basil, garlic, sea salt, and black pepper into a small blender and blend until smooth. Pour into a glass bowl, and slowly fold in the mayonnaise, olive oil, and grated cheese. Pour into a small glass jar. Set aside in cool place until ready to use.

Spicy Grilled Shrimp and Strawberry Salad with Spicy Strawberry Vinaigrette

PISTACHIOS ADD a wonderful crunch to the combination of shrimp and strawberries in this spicy, sweet, refreshing salad. Pistachio nuts have a delicate, subtle flavor and are a good source of calcium, thiamine, phosphorus, iron, and vitamin A.

16 fresh MSC-labeled Oregon pink shrimp
  (2 per person)
5 oz. spring greens
2 c. sugar snap peas
1 lb. fresh strawberries
½ bulb kohlrabi
2 ripe but firm avocados
½ c. green pistachios, roasted (see recipe on page 13)

1: **PREPARE THE VINAIGRETTE.**

2: **PREPARE SHRIMP.** Pour ¼ of the vinaigrette over the peeled shrimp, toss to coat, and marinate for 1 hour. Place shrimp on grilling skewers. To preheat the grill, set all burners on high heat, and close the lid. Heat for 10 minutes or until thermometer registers 500–550°F. Turn down to medium heat, and with the lid down, cook the shrimp 2 minutes on each side. Shrimp will turn pink when done. Let shrimp cool until read to assemble salad.

3: **PREPARE PRODUCE.** Wash and dry the spring greens. Wash, dry, and cut the sugar snap peas diagonally. Wash and dry the strawberries and then remove the stems and cut into fourths. Wash, dry, peel, and grate large the kohlrabi. Cut the avocados into uniform bite-sized pieces.

4: **ASSEMBLE SALAD.** Arrange half the greens on a pretty platter, sprinkle with half the shredded kohlrabi, half the pistachios, half the avocados, half the sugar snap peas, half the cooled shrimp, half the strawberries, and then repeat. Just before serving, drizzle Spicy Strawberry Vinaigrette over the salad.

Spicy Strawberry Vinaigrette

¼ c. rice vinegar
3 tbsp. strawberry preserves
4 tbsp. sweet Vidalia onion, minced
⅛ tsp. powdered allspice

¼ tsp. fresh lemon thyme
1 tsp. sea salt
1 tsp. finely ground black pepper
½ c. light and buttery-flavored olive oil
⅛ tsp. cayenne pepper

Place all ingredients except for cayenne into a small blender. Pulse-whirl together just until smooth and completely blended (about 10 seconds). Pour vinaigrette into a small glass jar. Cover and refrigerate until ready to make salad. Use ¼ c. vinaigrette with the cayenne pepper blended well for the shrimp marinade. Add the cayenne pepper a little at a time, and taste as you add.

Fresh Dandelion Greens Salad
with Scallion and Honey Bacon Vinaigrette

THIS SALAD IS BEST in early spring, before dandelion flowers emerge. Plan to harvest or purchase the dandelion greens at this time of year, when the leaves are still young and tender. Remember to use only organic dandelion greens.

8 thick-cut slices of hickory-smoked bacon

1½ lb. tender dandelion greens, tough stems removed

8 gold kiwi fruits, peeled and sliced in pretty rounds (they look like little dandelions)

1½ c. green pistachios, roasted (see recipe on page 13)

1: **COOK BACON.** In a medium skillet, cook bacon over medium heat, tossing occasionally until browned, 6–8 minutes. With a slotted spoon, transfer bacon to a towel-lined plate to drain. Set bacon aside to cool. After cooled, snip 7 slices diagonally into ¼-in. pieces. Crumble the other slice of bacon to use for the vinaigrette.

2: **PREPARE VINAIGRETTE.**

3: **ASSEMBLE SALADS.** Arrange dandelion greens on pretty salad plates or a platter for a crowd. Decorate the greens with snipped bacon and sliced golden kiwis, sprinkle with pistachios, and when vinaigrette is cooled down, spoon 2 tbsp. of dressing on each salad. Serve immediately.

Honey Bacon Vinaigrette

3 tbsp. of the bacon drippings and browned bits reserved in bacon pan

½ c. fruity green olive oil

½ c. scallions, chopped

¼ c. rice vinegar

4 tbsp. honey

1 tsp. Dijon mustard

1 tsp. sea salt

½ tsp. ground black pepper

1 strip bacon, nitrate free, if available

Pour off all but 3 tbsp. drippings from skillet. Return skillet to low heat, and carefully whisk in the olive oil. Add scallions, and cook for 30 seconds. Whisk in the vinegar, honey, Dijon mustard, salt, pepper, and crumbled bacon, scraping up the browned bits until the dressing is well combined. Cool about 10 minutes so that it is safe to spoon over plated salads.

Grilled Spring Lamb Chop and Fresh Arugula Salad with Apple Mint Vinaigrette

THIS IS MADE with haricot vert (pronounced ah-ree-koh VEHR), French for "little green bean." These slender beans have intense flavor with no "strings" to remove.

8 small red new potatoes, cleaned and quartered

1 tsp. sea salt

1 tsp. ground pepper

½ c. light gold olive oil (¼ c. for potatoes, and 2 tbsp. for lamb loin chops)

1 clove garlic, minced

1 tsp. grated lemon peel

8 lamb loin chops (Note: loin chops not lamb chops)

2 c. haricots verts, blanched

5 oz. baby arugula

½ c. SarVecchio Parmesan cheese, cut in ribbons

8 fresh sprigs of mint, for garnish

1: **PREPARE THE VINAIGRETTE.**

2: **PREPARE POTATOES.** Preheat oven to 450°F. Place potatoes in a mixing bowl. Sprinkle with ½ tsp. salt and ½ tsp. pepper. Add olive oil, and toss until potatoes are well coated. Spread potatoes out in a single layer on a baking pan. Roast for 40 minutes, or until potatoes are cooked through and browned, then cool.

3: **PREPARE LAMB LOIN CHOPS.** Combine olive oil, garlic, lemon zest, ½ tsp. salt, and ½ tsp. pepper in a bowl. Dip lamb chops into mixture to coat evenly. Cover chops and refrigerate for at least 30 minutes. Preheat the grill to 500–550°F. Turn down to medium-high heat, and with the lid down, cook the lamb chops about 5 minutes per side. Chops should be browned on both sides, slightly pink in the center. Remove from grill and cool until ready to compose salad.

4: **PREPARE HARICOTS VERTS.** Wash and cut off haricots verts tips. To blanch, bring 2 c. water to boil in a shallow pan, add the haricots verts, and turn off the burner. After 3 minutes, drain, and rinse with cold water to stop the cooking process. They should be bright green and tender crisp. Set aside.

5: **ASSEMBLE SALAD.** Arrange arugula in little mounds on 8 pretty salad plates, add a little lamb chop to each mound of arugula, arrange a small pile of the new potatoes and a little bundle of the haricots verts, then adorn with ribbons of SarVecchio cheese and a fresh little sprig of mint. Just before serving, drizzle salads with Apple Mint Vinaigrette.

Apple Mint Vinaigrette

¼ c. frozen apple juice concentrate

2 tbsp. rice vinegar

1 tbsp. Dijon mustard

½ tsp. sea salt

½ tsp. ground black pepper

2 tbsp. fresh mint, chopped

½ c. olive oil

Place all ingredients except olive oil in a small blender and blend until smooth. Pour into 1-qt. glass bowl and gently whisk in oil. Pour into small glass jar, cover, and refrigerate.

Garden Fresh Tabbouleh Salad with Zesty Lemon Vinaigrette

THE CHICKPEAS, sugar snap peas, grape tomatoes, and feta cheese in this recipe give a scrumptious new twist to the traditional tabbouleh. Serve this salad in a pretty, shallow salad bowl.

2 c. medium bulgur

1 c. water

2 tbsp. fresh lemon juice

2 c. dried chickpeas

1 c. fresh mint

2 c. flat parsley

1 c. scallions

1 c. sugar snap peas

2 c. heirloom grape tomatoes

1 c. Hidden Springs Farmstead Feta Cheese, **crumbled** (If Hidden Springs is not available, consult your cheesemonger for a comparable local feta cheese.)

1: **PREPARE THE VINAIGRETTE.**

2: **PREPARE BULGUR.** Pour bulgur into a 3-qt. glass mixing bowl, and pour approximately 1 c. water and 2 tbsp. fresh lemon juice over bulgur until bulgur is completely covered. Set aside until water is absorbed and the bulgur grains are soft (about 1–1½ hours). When soft, drain the bulgur grains completely.

3: **PREPARE CHICKPEAS.** Cook chickpeas, drain, and cool.

4: **PREPARE PRODUCE.** Wash and dry the mint, parsley, scallions, sugar snap peas, and grape tomatoes. Chop the produce (finely chop the scallions), and set aside.

5: **ASSEMBLE SALAD.** Add the Zesty Lemon Vinaigrette to the bulgur. Toss well and add in chopped parsley, mint, sugar snap peas, green onions, chickpeas, tomatoes, and feta. Toss again, and keep cold until ready to serve.

Zesty Lemon Vinaigrette

6 tbsp. fresh Meyer lemon juice

2 tbsp. local honey

2 tsp. Dijon mustard

½ clove garlic (More if you love it, but be careful not to overwhelm all the other wonderful spring flavors.)

1 tsp. sea salt

½ tsp. ground black pepper

½ c. olive oil

1 tbsp. lemon zest strips (thin julienne strips of lemon rind)

Pour lemon juice, honey, mustard, garlic, salt, and ground pepper into a small blender. Blend together until smooth. Pour into a bowl, and slowly whisk in olive oil and lemon zest. Blend until emulsified (completely combined). Set aside.

Memorial Day Quinoa Salad with Ginger Cherry Vinaigrette

SERVES 6–8

QUINOA, pronounced "keen-wah," has more protein than any other "grain" and cooks in minutes. Cooked quinoa seeds have a slightly nutty flavor with a texture that is creamy yet a little crunchy. Quinoa is considered a complete protein because it contains all eight essential amino acids, so this salad will give any meal a superb boost of nutrients.

2 c. red quinoa

4 c. water

2 c. red kale, removed from ribs and cut julienne

½ c. scallions, chopped

1 c. broccoli raab stems and flowers, chopped
  (also several broccoli raab blossoms if available)

1 c. frozen edamame, thawed and drained

1 c. dried cherries

1 c. roasted almonds (see recipe on page 13)

1: **PREPARE THE VINAIGRETTE.**

2: **PREPARE QUINOA.** Bring 4 c. water and 2 c. red quinoa to a boil, cover, and turn down the heat to low. Simmer for 15 minutes, then lift up the cover and stir. Quinoa should be firm but cooked through. The quinoa is done when the grain turns slightly transparent and the curly stringlike germ has separated from the circular part. Drain well, and set aside to cool.

3: **PREPARE PRODUCE.** Wash kale, trim leaves from center rib, and chop chiffonade (thin strips). Wash and chop scallions. Set aside.

4: **ASSEMBLE SALAD.** In a 3-qt. glass bowl or pretty, shallow salad bowl, combine the quinoa, kale, scallions, broccoli raab, edamame, scallions, cherries, and almonds. Garnish with broccoli raab blossoms, if available. Pour Ginger Cherry Vinaigrette onto salad, combine thoroughly, and serve.

Ginger Cherry Vinaigrette

¼ c. rice vinegar

3 tbsp. cherry preserves
  (or cherry whole fruit syrup, page 13)

1 tbsp. fresh ginger, peeled

½ clove fresh shallot or fresh garlic

1/8 tsp. sesame oil

1 tsp. sea salt

½ tsp. ground black pepper

½ c. olive oil

Put vinegar, cherry preserves, ginger, shallot/garlic, sesame oil, sea salt, and pepper into a small blender. Blend ingredients together until smooth, then pour these ingredients into a glass bowl, and slowly whisk in the olive oil until smooth and emulsified. Be careful not to whisk too much. Pour the vinaigrette into a small glass jar, and set aside in cool place until ready to use.

Beet Greens, Golden Beet, and Blueberry Salad à la mode with Savory Blueberry Vinaigrette

THIS NUTRITIOUS AND delicious salad uses the whole beet, from root to those lovely green leaves. Use a local chèvre, if available.

4–6 golden beets, roasted

2 tbsp. olive oil

5 oz. fresh beet greens (2 bunches of beets will make this amount)

2 c. fresh blueberries, washed and drained

1 c. fresh creamy chèvre cheese (Choose Stickney Hill Chèvre made in Minnesota, Pipers Pyramide Chèvre made in Indiana, or another chèvre goat cheese if made closer to your home.)

½ c. roasted walnuts (see page 13)

Cracked black pepper

1: **PREPARE THE VINAIGRETTE.**

2: **PREPARE BEETS.** Preheat the oven to 350°F. Wash the beets thoroughly, remove greens, and leave the skins on. Rinse greens, removing any large stems, and set aside. Place the beets in a small baking dish or roasting pan, and toss with 2 tbsp. of olive oil. Cover, and bake for 45–60 minutes, or until a knife can slide easily through the largest beet. Remove from oven and cool. Peel each beet, wipe clean, and cut into little golden half moons. Set aside.

3: **PREPARE BEET GREENS.** Trim stems off leaves, tear beet greens into large bite-sized pieces, and set aside.

4: **ASSEMBLE SALAD.** Arrange beet greens on each of 8 salad plates, fan the golden beets on top of the greens, and sprinkle with blueberries. With a small melon scooper, scoop a little teaspoon-sized ball of chèvre onto each group of golden beets, à la mode style. Sprinkle with walnuts and cracked pepper. Just before serving, drizzle with Savory Blueberry Vinaigrette.

Savory Blueberry Vinaigrette

¼ c. rice vinegar

2 tbsp. blueberry preserves (or blueberry whole fruit syrup, page 13)

1 tsp. Dijon mustard

1 tsp. sweet onion, minced

1 tsp. sea salt

½ tsp. ground black pepper

½ c. fruity green olive oil

Place all vinaigrette ingredients except for olive oil in a small blender. Pulse-whirl together until smooth and completely blended, pour into 1-qt. glass bowl, and gently whisk in olive oil. Don't whisk too long, as it will get too thick. Pour vinaigrette into small glass jar, cover, and refrigerate until ready to make salad.

Wild Crab-Stuffed Artichoke Salad with Lemon Tarragon Dressing

A HOLLOWED ARTICHOKE is an artful, elegant container for any number of salad combinations. The fresh flavors of crab salad with Lemon Tarragon Dressing make this a tasty spring treat.

2 lb. Dungeness crabmeat (wild-caught from California, Oregon, or Washington)

1 c. tiny shelled peas

1 c. sweet red bell pepper, chopped fine

8 whole artichokes

2 tbsp. lemon juice (for the artichoke steaming water)

1 tbsp. lemon zest (for garnish)

8 fresh tarragon sprigs (for garnish)

1: **PREPARE THE DRESSING.**

2: **PREPARE CRABMEAT SALAD.** Mix together crabmeat, peas, and red bell peppers with Lemon Tarragon Dressing. Combine well, and refrigerate until artichokes are cool enough to stuff.

3: **PREPARE ARTICHOKES.** Wash artichokes thoroughly by holding the stem and swishing and tapping upside down to be sure to clean inside the leaves. Cut the long stem off to about 1 in. so the artichoke can easily stand in the pan (the stem is edible, so don't cut too much). Cut about 1 in. off the top of the artichoke with a serrated knife. Put prepared artichoke in a pan filled with 2 in. of cool water with fresh lemon juice until you are ready to steam. Cover pot and steam artichokes for about 30–40 minutes (depending on size), or until bottoms of the artichoke are tender (test with a fork). Check the water level often, as it's easy to forget about and let boil dry. Drain carefully and rinse with cool water.

Put artichokes on a clean, dry towel, dry, and cool. Using a grapefruit spoon or melon baller, hollow out the middle, including the hairy choke (make sure you remove all of this).

4: **ASSEMBLE SALAD.** Stand each artichoke upright on a clean counter, making sure they stand up easily and are sturdy. You may have to cut the bottom of the stems a bit to flatten your artichoke bottom so it will stand and not topple over. Mince any stem you cut off, and put it in the crab salad. Divide crab salad between the 8 artichokes. Garnish with lemon zest and tarragon leaf, and serve.

Lemon Tarragon Dressing

4 tbsp. fresh lemon juice

3 tbsp. honey

4 tbsp. fresh tarragon, chopped fine

2 tbsp. red onion, chopped

½ tsp. sea salt

½ tsp. black pepper

¼ c. olive oil

2 c. mayonnaise

2 c. SarVecchio Asiago cheese, grated

1 tsp. lemon zest

Place lemon juice, honey, tarragon, red onion, sea salt, black pepper, and olive oil in a small blender. Pulse-whirl together until smooth, and pour into a 1-qt. glass bowl. Gently fold in the mayonnaise, cheese, and lemon zest.

Baby Greens and Fava Beans Salad with Simple Spring Vinaigrette

SERVES 6–8

FRESH FAVA BEANS are a sure sign of spring, and this salad is best made with just-picked beans. At the farmers' market, look for pods that are not bulging with beans; this indicates older beans and subpar flavor.

16 fresh fava bean pods

⅛ tsp. sea salt

2 tsp. walnut oil

½ c. shaved ¼-in. ribbons of fresh fennel bulb

5 oz. mixed baby greens, washed and dried

1 c. Ladysmith cheese, grated (Ladysmith cheese is made by the Samish Bay Creamery in Washington State and is similar to an Italian ricotta salata. If it is not available, ask your cheesemonger for a comparable local cheese.)

½ c. walnuts

2 tbsp. fresh fennel greens

6–8 pansy blossoms (yellow)

1: **PREPARE** the Simple Spring Vinaigrette on page 16.

2: **PREPARE FAVA BEANS.** Shell the fava beans as you would a pod of fresh peas. Rinse gently. Bring 3 c. water to a boil in a shallow pan, pour in beans, reduce heat, and simmer for 3 minutes. Remove from stove and rinse with cold water to cool. When cool, carefully remove the fava bean skin (the little light green jacket) from the beautiful, bright green fava seed. Place seeds in a little bowl, and cover with ⅛ tsp. sea salt and 2 tbsp. walnut oil. Set aside for salad assembly.

3: **PREPARE FENNEL BULB.** Slice off the stems and the dirty, hard base at the bottom of your bulb. Don't slice too far into the bulb itself, or the fennel will be more difficult for you to slice. Like an onion, fennel's base is what holds the layers. Cut the bulb in half lengthwise. If it's an especially large bulb of fennel, you may wish to cut it into quarters as well. Slice the fennel thinly and evenly with your knife, and set aside.

4: **ASSEMBLE SALAD.** Arrange greens on a pretty platter or divide among salad plates, and sprinkle greens with cheese, walnuts, fennel shavings, and fava beans. Sprinkle with chopped fennel greens, and decorate with an edible pansy on each plate or scatter on the large salad. Just before serving, drizzle each salad with the Simple Spring Vinaigrette.

Buy Organic

Lettuce ranks number 13 on the list of produce with the highest pesticide loads, according to the Environmental Working Group, ww.foodnews.org. For further research, you can go to www.whatsonmyfood.com. Buying organic or growing your own lettuce are good options. Lettuce is easily grown in a window box. Many varieties can even grow indoors. Check out www.organicgardening.com or www.gardeningknowhow.com for further information.

Summer Salads

TO ME, summer days mean salad days! Being able to pick fresh herbs and greens from my own garden is the best. When I want further inspiration, I simply stroll through my local farmers' market—a trip to market without a list in hand is my idea of true summer serendipity, which often leads to the most inspired salad creations.

Summer gives salad lovers reason to celebrate, as so many of the local farmers are planting amazing varieties of heirloom lettuces and bitter greens. Every week at market, something new seems to ripen— greens, berries, peas, beans, baby golden beets, glorious summer squashes, heirloom tomatoes galore, and always some new vegetable that I've never seen or tasted before. I love to take advantage of these unusual offerings by heading right to my kitchen to create a new artisan salad, filled with all of my newly found ingredients. We open the doors, picnic alfresco, enjoy good company, and share the season's bounty.

Mango Tango Salad with Chili Lime Vinaigrette

TANGO LETTUCE HAS frilly leaves and a mild, tangy taste. With a bright golden green color, Tango leaves make for a gorgeous salad, especially when paired with a red lettuce, such as Redina or Marvel of Four Seasons. Look for Tango lettuce at farmers' markets.

4 cornbread muffins or 4 ¼-in.-thick slices cornbread (for chipotle cornbread croutons)

2 tbsp. olive oil

¼ tsp. sea salt

½ tsp. chili powder

6–8 chicken breasts

2 c. black beans

7 oz. fresh tango lettuce

8 ripe mangos

4 ripe avocados

2 c. raw sweet corn (fresh from the cob)

1 c. queso fresco cheese, finely grated

1 c. roasted pecans (see recipe on page 13)

1: PREPARE VINAIGRETTE.

2: PREPARE CORNBREAD CROUTONS. Preheat oven to 300°F. Cut cornbread muffins or slices into ¼-in. cubes, gently brush all sides with olive oil, place on a baking sheet, sprinkle with sea salt and chili powder, and toast in oven for 20 minutes or until golden brown and crunchy. Set aside to cool.

3: PREPARE CHICKEN. To preheat the grill before cooking, set all burners on high heat, and close the lid. Heat for 10 minutes or until thermometer registers 500–550°F. Turn down to medium heat, and with the lid down, cook chicken 6½ minutes per side or until the meat thermometer reads 160°F. Let the chicken cool and then julienne-slice.

4: PREPARE PRODUCE. Cook, drain, and cool black beans. Wash and thoroughly dry tango lettuce. Wash, skin, and slice mangos and avocados into julienne strips. Shuck corn and cut raw corn off the cob.

5: ASSEMBLE SALAD. Divide and arrange washed and dried tango leaves among 6–8 plates, and sprinkle with black beans, cheese, and corn. Divide and arrange chicken slices, sliced avocados, and sliced mangos on each salad. Arrange croutons on each salad, and sprinkle with pecans. Just before serving, drizzle with Chili Lime Vinaigrette.

Chili Lime Vinaigrette

2½ tbsp. honey

¾ c. fresh lime juice

2 tbsp. sweet onion, minced

1 tbsp. cilantro, minced

2 tsp. sea salt

½ tsp. chili powder

½ tsp. finely ground black pepper

⅛ tsp. lime zest

1 c. olive oil

Pour honey, lime juice, onion, cilantro, sea salt, chili powder, ground pepper, and lime zest into a small blender and blend completely. Pour into a bowl, and slowly whisk in the olive oil until thoroughly combined. Pour into a glass jar, cover, and keep cool until ready to assemble salad.

Summer "Sea-sar" Salad
with Creamy Lemony Dill Caesar Dressing

PUT THE "SEA" IN this Caesar's Salad with some delicious Oregon pink shrimp. If you prefer to use lobster or scallops, choose a sustainable variety that's included on the Monterey Bay Aquarium's "Best Choices" list, such as U.S. spiny lobsters and scallops that have been farmed off the bottom of oceans.

4 slices of sourdough bread

2 tbsp. olive oil

1 tsp. dried dill

⅛ tsp. sea salt

¼ c. SarVecchio Parmesan cheese, finely grated (If SarVecchio is not available, ask your cheesemonger for a similar tasting, local cheese.)

8 oz. romaine lettuce

½ c. green onions, chopped

24 cherry or grape heirloom tomatoes

32 large Oregon pink shrimp (4 per serving), cooked, cleaned, and chilled (Note: 2 c. cooked lobster meat cut in bite-sized pieces and 2 c. sautéed sea scallops could be used instead)

1: **PREPARE THE DRESSING.**

2: **PREPARE CROUTONS.** Preheat oven to 250°F. Cut sourdough bread slices into ¼-in. squares, put into a large glass bowl, brush all sides with 2 tbsp. extra-virgin olive oil, and then sprinkle with dried dill, sea salt, and cheese. Toss well to cover each crouton. Spread onto a cookie sheet, and toast for 20–25 minutes, until golden and crunchy. Set aside.

3: **PREPARE PRODUCE.** Wash and thoroughly dry the produce. Cut lettuce into bite-sized pieces, chop onions (bulb and greens), and cut tomatoes in halves.

4: **ASSEMBLE SALAD.** Combine the cooked, chilled shrimp with ½ c. Creamy Lemony Dill Caesar Dressing, and set aside. In a large 3-qt. glass or wooden bowl, combine the romaine lettuce, shrimp, green onions, croutons, and remaining dressing. Toss gently together, then divide onto 8 dinner plates and decorate with little tomatoes and the remaining shrimp (4 per salad). Sprinkle with cracked pepper, and serve right way.

Creamy Lemony Dill Caesar Dressing

3 tbsp. honey

½ c. fresh lemon juice

½ clove garlic

1 tsp. Dijon mustard

2 tsp. sea salt

1 tsp. black pepper

½ c. extra-virgin olive oil

1½ c. olive oil–based mayonnaise

1 tbsp. fresh dill weed, rinsed and patted dry

1 tsp. finely grated lemon zest

¾ c. parmesan cheese, finely grated

In a small blender, combine honey, lemon juice, garlic, mustard, sea salt, and black pepper. Pour into a glass bowl, and slowly whisk in the oil. Gently fold in the mayonnaise, fresh dill, lemon zest, and finely grated cheese.

Heirloom Tomato Salad
with Creamy Buttermilk Asiago Dressing

THIS SALAD IS BEST made at the peak of tomato season with the freshest tomatoes you can find. Look for just-picked, local heirloom tomatoes at farmers' markets and farm stands. **NOTE:** Choose 3 different colors, shapes, and varieties of heirloom tomatoes from the market.

8 slices day-old French baguette for croutons

½ c. olive oil

1 tbsp. SarVecchio Asiago cheese, finely grated (or comparable asiago cheese)

Fresh-ground black pepper

8 oz. escarole lettuce

4 greenish or striped heirloom tomatoes (such as Green Zebra)

4 yellow heirloom tomatoes (such as Golden Nugget)

4 red heirloom tomatoes (such as Brandywine)

¼ c. red onion, sliced into rings

1: **PREPARE DRESSING.**

2: **PREPARE CROUTONS.** Preheat oven to 250°F. Cut baguette into ¼-in. squares, put squares in big glass bowl, and toss with ½ c. extra-virgin olive oil. Sprinkle and toss with asiago cheese and ground pepper. Pour onto a baking sheet and toast for 20–25 minutes, until golden and crunchy. Set aside to let cool.

3: **PREPARE TOMATOES, ONION, AND LETTUCE.** Wash, thoroughly dry, and tear the lettuce into bite-sized pieces. Wash and cut the tomatoes into uniform bite-sized chunks. Cut the onion into rings, and cut each ring into fourths.

4: **ASSEMBLE SALAD.** Arrange escarole on a pretty 9x18-in. platter, and decorate with heirloom tomatoes and red onions. Sprinkle with half the croutons. Place the remaining croutons in a little bowl with a serving spoon and place it next to the salad platter along with a pitcher of the Creamy Buttermilk Asiago Dressing.

Creamy Buttermilk Asiago Dressing

2 tbsp. honey

2 tbsp. rice vinegar

2 tbsp. fresh chives, chopped

1 tsp. sea salt

1 tsp. ground black pepper

¼ c. extra-virgin olive oil

1½ c. olive oil–based mayonnaise

¼ c. buttermilk

½ c. asiago, finely grated

Put honey, rice vinegar, fresh chives, sea salt, black pepper, and olive oil in small blender, and blend until smooth. Pour mixture into a glass bowl, and slowly fold in the mayonnaise, buttermilk, and grated cheese. Mix all together, pour into a small glass jar, and set aside in a cool place.

Grilled Grass-Fed Steak Salad
with Creamy Cowboy Ranch Dressing

FOR THIS RECIPE, look for steak tenderloins with the USDA Organic label, which ensures the cows were raised without any growth hormones or antibiotics and that their feed was not grown with pesticides or fertilizers.

4 thick-cut slices grainy and seedy whole-wheat bread

2 tbsp. butter, softened

¼ c. San Andreas cheese (or another pecorino-style cheese), finely grated

1 lb. green string beans

7 oz. romaine lettuce leaves

4–5 large heirloom beefsteak-type tomatoes

4 1-lb. grilled beef tenderloin steaks

1: **PREPARE DRESSING.**

2: **PREPARE CROUTONS.** Preheat oven to 300°F. Butter both sides of bread, and sprinkle with grated cheese. Place on a baking sheet, and toast for 10 minutes per side until semi-toasty and cheese is melted. Remove from oven, and set aside until you are finished grilling steaks. When steaks are done, set aside to cool, and turn off the grill. Transfer each slice of bread to the grill with metal tongs. Count to 10 and turn clockwise, repeat until all slices are grilled on both sides. Let cool, and with a serrated knife, cut into ½-in. cubes for croutons. Set aside.

3: **PREPARE GREEN BEANS.** Cut the tips off the bean heads and carefully rinse the string beans. Drain in colander and blanch in boiling, salted water for 3–4 minutes. Remove the beans to a bowl of ice water to chill for at least 10 minutes. Pat dry, and set aside in a cool place.

Creamy Cowboy Ranch Dressing

2 tbsp. maple syrup

3 tbsp. rice vinegar

1 tsp. Dijon mustard

2 tbsp. red onion, minced

1 tbsp. chili powder

⅛ tsp. ground chipotle powder (or ½ tsp. chili powder)

½ tbsp. fresh chopped chives

½ tbsp. fresh thyme

½ tbsp. chopped basil

2 tsp. sea salt

1 tsp. ground black pepper

¼ c. extra-virgin olive oil

2 c. olive oil–based mayonnaise

½ c. fresh sour cream

Put maple syrup, rice vinegar, Dijon mustard, onion, chili powder, chipotle powder, chives, thyme, basil, sea salt, black pepper, and olive oil into a small blender, and blend together until smooth. Pour these ingredients into a glass bowl and slowly whisk in the mayonnaise and sour cream. Pour into a glass jar, and set aside in cool place until ready to use.

continued on page 58

Shopping 4-1-1

When you purchase your steak tenderloins, look for meat that was raised and processed closest to your home. This cuts down on the environmental impact of transportation and allows you to ask meat managers and farmers more questions directly. Many meats are sold at farmers' markets, and many farmers make weekly home deliveries. For further information, consult www.organicconsumers.org or go to www.greenerchoices.org (a *Consumer Reports* website). You will find a Meat, Dairy, and Eggs Buying Guide within the "Green Shopping" heading and the "Food" subheading.

4: **PREPARE TOMATOES AND ROMAINE.** Wash and thoroughly dry the romaine lettuce. Use the crisp inner leaves. Wash the tomatoes and cut into 4 round slices. Cut the slices into uniform halves, and sprinkle with salt and pepper.

5: **GRILL STEAKS.** Remove steaks from the refrigerator 20 minutes before grilling so that they are closer to room temperature. Rub each side with olive oil, sea salt, and pepper. Preheat the grill to 500–550°F. Sear steak on high for 4 minutes per side, then turn down to medium and grill 4 minutes per side until thermometer reads 150°F for "medium" (slightly pink inside). Flip steaks with tongs instead of a fork to prevent loss of valuable juices. When the steaks have cooled, use a very sharp knife to cut the meat into ¼-in. julienned slices. Set aside in a cool place until ready to assemble the salad.

6: **ASSEMBLE SALAD.** Choose 8 dinner-sized plates, and arrange 4–6 whole romaine leaves on each plate. Divide the green beans evenly, arranging them on top of the romaine. Fan 4 tomato slices on the romaine, and divide the steak between the plates (approximately ½ tenderloin per person, 5–6 thin slices), fanning the slices on top of the tomato slices. Place the Texas toast croutons in a little neat little stack on top of the steak and, just before serving, drizzle with the Creamy Cowboy Ranch Dressing. Serve extra dressing in a little pitcher with a spoon and enjoy.

Peachy Keen Salad with Peach Vinaigrette

SWEET, JUICY, TANGY, and succulent, peaches are the perfect summer treat. In this recipe, a freestone peach is featured (it has flesh that is easily removed from the stone, or pit, of the fruit). It is usually larger, firmer, and less juicy, but very sweet when compared to its clingstone cousins.

7 oz. red and green leaf lettuce

1 c. red onions

4 ripe but firm freestone peaches (see cutting suggestions below)

1 c. Marcona almonds (whole fair trade nuts if possible)

½ c. Solé GranQueso cheese, grated (If Solé GranQueso is not available, ask your cheesemonger for a similar-tasting, local cheese.)

1: **PREPARE DRESSING.**

2: **PREPARE PRODUCE.** Wash and thoroughly dry the lettuce. Remove the skins and thinly slice the red onions.

3: **CUT PEACHES.** Gently wash and dry fruit. With a sharp knife, cut a slab of fresh fruit off each side of the pit (also called the stone of the fruit). Flip the fruit, and cut the smaller sides of the fruit off the pit also. Lay the two large slabs facedown on a cutting board, and slice into 4 uniform slices. Cut the smaller slabs to match.

4: **ASSEMBLE SALAD.** Arrange lettuce leaves on 8 pretty summer salad plates, place slices of peach on top of greens in a fan, and sprinkle with Marcona almonds and cheese. Just before serving, drizzle with Peach Vinaigrette.

Peach Vinaigrette

3 tbsp. peach preserves
¼ c. rice vinegar
1 tsp. sweet onion, minced
1 tsp. Dijon mustard
1½ tsp. sea salt
½ tsp. ground black pepper
½ c. fruity green olive oil

Place all dressing ingredients except for olive oil in a small blender. Blend together until smooth and completely blended. Pour into 1-qt. glass bowl, and gently whisk in olive oil until combined. Pour dressing into a glass jar, cover, and refrigerate until ready to make salad.

Buy It Organic

Peaches have the second-highest pesti-cide load for produce, according to the research of the Environmental Working Group. For more information, go to www.foodnews.org. Purchasing organic peaches that are grown closest to your home is the "green" way to go. For further research, go to the Pesticide Action Network's website at www.whatsonmyfood.com.

Summer Shore Salad with Sweet Onion and Tarragon Dressing

SERVES 6–8

THIS SALAD IS THE next best thing to catching your own fresh trout and cooking it over a campfire. I recommend brown sugar smoked rainbow trout filets from a local source, if available.

6–8 brown sugar smoked rainbow trout filets, nitrite free, if available

7 oz. microgreens (if available) or mixed baby greens

2 red tomatoes

2 yellow tomatoes

2 c. fresh sugar snap peas

1 c. ribbons shaved SarVecchio Parmesan cheese (or a comparable local cheese)

8 sprigs fresh tarragon

1: **PREPARE DRESSING.**

2: **PREPARE TROUT.** Carefully remove skin from pieces of trout and then remove any bones from flesh of trout. Pull trout into bite-sized pieces, and keep refrigerated until ready to compose salad.

3: **PREPARE PRODUCE.** Wash and dry microgreens or mixed baby greens. Wash and cut the tomatoes into ¼-in. chunks. Wash the sugar snap peas, and cut diagonally into bite-sized pieces.

4: **ASSEMBLE SALAD.** Among 6–8 dinner plates, divide microgreens and then place pieces of trout evenly on the greens. Decorate with tomatoes, sugar snap peas, and the ribbons of cheese. With a tbsp., place a dollop of dressing on each salad and then add a sprig of fresh tarragon. Serve the extra dressing in a little pitcher on the side.

Sweet Onion and Tarragon Dressing

1 tbsp. sweet Vidalia onion, minced
¼ c. fresh lemon juice
¼ c. fresh heavy cream
2 tbsp. fresh tarragon
2 tbsp. honey
1 tsp. sea salt
½ tsp. ground black pepper
1½ c. olive oil–based mayonnaise

Put onion, lemon juice, heavy cream, tarragon, honey, sea salt, and pepper into blender, and whirl until combined and smooth. Pour into a deep 2-qt. glass bowl, and gently whisk with mayonnaise. Keep cool.

Star Prairie Trout Farm

Since 1856, Star Prairie Trout Farm in Wisconsin has provided an ideal natural habitat for commercial trout raising. The trout are raised on pure feed without additives or medication in pristine, 100 percent spring water. The farm delivers fresh rainbow trout twice a week to local co-ops and farmers' markets. Purchasing from small, local fish farms with sustainable practices is the best choice. Look for a trout farm near you at www.localharvest.org.

Plum Great Salad with Plum and Cilantro Vinaigrette

YOU WILL BE DELIGHTED with the contrasting flavors in this salad—the plums, gouda, and cilantro taste great together. Choose a variety of different-colored plums for the best presentation.

8 slices grainy honey whole-wheat bread

2 tbsp. olive oil

1½ c. Goodhue Grass-Fed Gouda Cheese, grated large (Reserve 1 tbsp. for croutons)

Cracked black pepper

5–7 oz. fresh arugula

16 whole cilantro leaves with ½-in. stems

9 ripe plums (3 each of a different color and variety)

1½ c. roasted pecans (see recipe on page 13)

1: **PREPARE VINAIGRETTE.**

2: **CREATE CILANTRO LEAF-SHAPED CROUTONS.** Trace the leaf illustration shown on page 91 and cut out a template for cutting croutons. Preheat oven to 250°F. Lay out slices of bread on cutting board. Using the leaf template, gently cut out the leaf shape with a small, sharp paring knife tip (two leaves per slice of bread). Brush each side of the bread leaf with olive oil, arrange leaves on cookie sheet, and sprinkle with a pinch of gouda cheese and a crack of black pepper. Toast in the oven for 10 minutes. Pull out of oven, and carefully place a clover of cilantro on each leaf. Press in gently and return to oven for another 10 minutes. The cilantro should be a bit darker. Remove from oven and cool before assembling salad.

3: **PREPARE PRODUCE.** Wash and thoroughly dry the arugula. Rinse and pat dry the cilantro leavess.

4: **PREPARE PLUMS.** Wash and dry the plums. With a sharp knife, cut a slab of fresh fruit off each side of pit (the stone of the fruit). Flip the fruit, and cut the smaller sides of the fruit off the pit also. Lay the two large slabs facedown on cutting board, and cut into 4 uniform wedges. Cut the smaller slabs to match.

5: **ASSEMBLE THE SALAD.** Divide arugula among 8 pretty salad plates, sprinkle with cheese, decorate with plums. Place 2 cilantro crouton leaves on the edge of the arugula on each plate (like the leaves on a corsage), and sprinkle with pecans. Just before serving, drizzle salads with Plum and Cilantro Vinaigrette.

Plum and Cilantro Vinaigrette

2 tbsp. plum preserves

¼ c. rice vinegar

1 tbsp. fresh cilantro

1 tsp. sweet onion

1 tsp. stone-ground mustard

1 tsp. sea salt

½ tsp. pepper

½ c. fruity green olive oil

Place all vinaigrette ingredients except for olive oil in a small blender and blend until smooth. Pour into a 1-qt. glass bowl, and gently whisk in olive oil. Pour into a glass jar, cover, and refrigerate.

Red, White, and Blueberry Salad with Pink Lemonade Vinaigrette

SERVES 6-8

BLUEBERRIES ARE A DELECTABLE summer treat rich in antioxidants, fiber, and vitamin C. The combination of blueberries, raspberries, chèvre, and almonds in this patriotic salad is a flavor sensation. Serve on a large decorative platter with a meal at home or in a shallow woven basket lined with a flour sack towel at a party.

7 oz. mixed greens

2 c. sugar snap peas

2 c. blueberries

2 c. raspberries

1 c. chèvre, crumbled (If you choose a log or cake of chèvre, freeze it until it is firm and then crumble it. Choose Stickney Hill Chèvre made in Minnesota, Hoja Santa Chèvre made in Texas, or another chèvre goat cheese if made closer to your home.)

1 c. roasted almonds (see recipe on page 13)

1: **PREPARE VINAIGRETTE.**

2: **PREPARE PRODUCE.** Wash and thoroughly dry the greens and sugar snap peas. Cut the peas diagonally in half. Rinse and dry the blueberries, and just before assembling the salad, gently rinse and delicately pat dry the raspberries.

3: **ASSEMBLE SALAD.** Line a pretty, shallow woven basket platter (8x14 in. and 2–4 in. deep) with a clean, ironed, white flour sack towel, or use a large, decorative salad platter. Arrange your salad ingredients in "layered salad style": half greens, half cheese, half nuts, half blueberries, half raspberries, and half sugar snap peas, then repeat. Just before serving, drizzle Pink Lemonade Vinaigrette over the salad. Serve with tongs.

Pink Lemonade Vinaigrette

2 tbsp. raspberry preserves (The raspberry whole fruit syrup on page 13 is delicious and perfect for this recipe.)

4 tbsp. lemon juice

1 tsp. sweet Vidalia onion, minced

1 tsp. Dijon mustard

1 tsp. sea salt

½ tsp. ground black pepper

½ c. light-colored and buttery mild olive oil

Place all vinaigrette ingredients except for olive oil in a small blender. Blend together until smooth and completely blended. Pour into a 1-qt. glass bowl, and gently whisk in the olive oil. Don't whisk too long, as it will get too thick. Pour vinaigrette into a glass jar, cover, and refrigerate until ready to assemble salad.

Blueberries

Choose organic blueberries that are dry, plump, firm, and uniform in size with a soft, hazy white coating. Store blueberries unwashed in a single layer in a moisture-proof container in the refrigerator for up to 5 days. If you purchase extra blueberries locally during the peak season, you can freeze them and enjoy later.

Bitter Greens and Golden Berry Salad with Balsamic and Vanilla Bean Vinaigrette

THE MELLOW, SWEET, vanilla-flavored vinaigrette tames the sharpness of the bitter greens, making this simple salad a favorite in mid-summer, when raspberries are at their peak.

7 oz. mixed bitter greens (Choose a combination of bitter greens, such as frisée, Belgian endive, radicchio chicory, or baby mustard greens.)

2–3 c. golden raspberries

½ c. dried currants

1½ c. SarVecchio Parmesan cheese, (or a comparable local cheese) grated

1 c. roasted walnuts (see recipe on page 13)

1: **PREPARE THE VINAIGRETTE.**

2: **PREPARE PRODUCE.** Wash and thoroughly dry the greens. Just before assembling the salad, gently rinse and pat dry the raspberries.

3: **ASSEMBLE SALAD.** Divide and arrange bitter greens among 8 pretty salad plates, sprinkle greens with cheese, golden raspberries, currants, and walnuts. Just before serving, drizzle with Balsamic and Vanilla Bean Vinaigrette.

Balsamic and Vanilla Bean Vinaigrette

Seeds scraped from one pod of vanilla bean (approximately ⅟₁₆ tsp.)	1 tsp. Dijon mustard
	1 tsp. sea salt
4 tbsp. balsamic vinegar	¼ tsp. ground black pepper
1 tsp. chopped shallot	½ c. golden fruity olive oil
2 tbsp. clover honey	

Soften the vanilla pod by steaming it for 1–2 minutes in a steamer or in a sieve over boiling water. Let it cool slightly. It will be much easier to slit. Scrape the seeds out over a sheet of parchment paper or waxed paper. If you don't use the paper, you will lose some of the precious seeds, as they will cling to your hands or even get under your fingernails as you try to pick them up. Put the vanilla seed paste, balsamic vinegar, shallot, honey, mustard, salt, and ground pepper into a small blender. Blend together just until the ingredients are completely combined. Pour these ingredients into a glass mixing bowl. Slowly whisk in the olive oil, and combine well. Put into a glass jar, and keep cool until ready to serve.

Grilled Wild Salmon and Red Raspberry Salad with Pink Peppercorn and Raspberry Vinaigrette

SALMON IS AN EXCELLENT source of omega-3 fatty acids that may improve heart health. The Monterey Bay Aquarium recommends wild-caught, Alaskan salmon rather than farmed salmon. Refer to www.mbayaq.org for more information.

8 salmon filets (1-in. thick, 6 oz. each)

olive oil

salt

pepper

7 oz. fresh arugula

½ c. chèvre cheese, crumbled (If you choose a log or cake of chèvre, freeze it until it is firm and then crumble it. Choose Stickney Hill Chèvre made in Minnesota, Cypress Grove Chevre made in California, or another chèvre if made closer to your home.)

2 c. fresh raspberries

½ c. roasted hazelnuts (see recipe on page 13)

1: **PREPARE THE VINAIGRETTE.**

2: **GRILL SALMON.** Brush each side of salmon with olive oil and salt and pepper. Carefully, with a thick cloth, wipe the grill grates with olive oil also. Preheat burners on high 10 minutes, then turn down to medium, and put salmon on grill skin side down. Cover, and cook 5 minutes on one side and then flip with a metal spatula. Cook covered for another 5 minutes to grill "medium." Transfer to a platter, and let cool a bit before you assemble salads.

3: **WASH AND THOROUGHLY DRY** the arugula. Gently rinse the raspberries right before assembling the salad.

4: **ASSEMBLE SALAD.** Pick out eight summery dinner plates, and arrange a bed of fresh arugula on each plate. Sprinkle with half the goat cheese crumbles and half the crumbled hazelnuts. Place a salmon filet on each bed of arugula, decorate with raspberries, remaining goat cheese, and crumbled hazelnuts. Drizzle with vinaigrette, and serve right away.

Pink Peppercorn and Raspberry Vinaigrette

3 tbsp. raspberry preserves	½ tsp. pink peppercorns
¼ c. balsamic vinegar	1 tsp. stone-ground mustard
1 tsp. sea salt	½ c. fruity olive oil

Put raspberry preserves, balsamic vinegar, sea salt, pink peppercorns, and stone-ground mustard into a small blender. Blend ingredients together just to combine, and pour these ingredients into a glass bowl. Slowly whisk in the olive oil until combined and emulsified. Pour into a glass jar, cover, and keep cool until ready to serve salad.

Nectarine and Nasturtium Salad with Simple Summer Vinaigrette

NASTURTIUMS ARE edible annual flowers that range in color from dark orange to yellow. Harvest the edible leaves when they are young, as the older leaves can be bitter. Nasturtiums are related to the cress family and have a slight peppery taste. The beautiful blossoms (edible but with less taste than the leaves) make this fresh, fruity salad an aesthetic delight.

7 oz. arugula

Garden-fresh nasturtium leaves

4 firm but ripe nectarines

1 c. Goat Gouda cheese, grated (Reserve 1 tbsp. for croutons. We recommend Goodhue Grass-fed Gouda. If it is not available, ask your cheese monger for a similar local Gouda.)

1 c. roasted hazelnuts (see recipe on page 13)

8 small nasturtium blossoms

Simple Summer Vinaigrette

2 tbsp. summer wildflower honey
6 tbsp. rice vinegar
1 tsp. Dijon mustard
1 tsp. sea salt
½ tsp. fine-ground black pepper
½ c. light golden olive oil

Put honey, rice vinegar, mustard, salt, and ground pepper into a small blender. Blend ingredients together to completely combine. Pour into a bowl, and slowly whisk in the olive oil until thoroughly combined. Pour into a glass jar, cover, and keep cool until ready to assemble salad.

1: **PREPARE VINAIGRETTE.**

2: **PREPARE PRODUCE.** Wash and thoroughly dry the greens. Gently rinse, pat dry, and remove the stems from the nasturtium leaves.

3: **PREPARE NECTARINES.** Wash and dry fruit and then with sharp knife, cut a slab of fresh fruit off each side of pit (the stone of the fruit). Flip fruit, and cut the smaller sides of the fruit off the pit, too. Lay the 2 large slabs facedown on cutting board, and slice into 4 uniform slices. Cut the smaller slabs to match, creating 8–10 pretty and uniform slices.

4: **ASSEMBLE SALAD.** Mix arugula and nasturtium leaves together, and divide among 8 little salad plates or teacups. Sprinkle with cheese, nectarines, and nuts, and decorate with nasturtium blossoms. Just before serving, drizzle each salad with the Simple Summer Vinaigrette.

Grilled Veggies and Cheese Tortellini Salad with Basil and Sun-Dried Tomato Vinaigrette

GRILLING BRINGS OUT the natural flavors and sweetness of the squash, zucchini, and peppers, making this tortellini salad phenomenal.

20 oz. three-cheese tortellini

1 c. fresh basil

2 c. fresh, ripe tomatoes

1 yellow summer squash

1 green zucchini

1 red bell pepper

1 yellow bell pepper

4 large portobello mushrooms

4 whole green onions

6 tbsp. olive oil

Sea salt and pepper to season

2 c. Crave Brothers Fresh Mozzarella, grated (or a comparable local cheese)

1 c. SarVecchio Parmesan, grated (or a similar local cheese)

2 c. roasted pistachios (see recipe on page 13)

1: **PREPARE VINAIGRETTE.**

2: **PREPARE TORTELLINI.** Cook tortellini according to al dente cooking instructions, drain, and rinse with cool water to stop cooking process. Set aside to cool.

3: **PREPARE PRODUCE AND GRILL VEGETABLES.** Rinse the basil, gently pat dry, and chop. Wash the tomatoes and chop. Set basil and tomatoes aside. Wash and cut summer squash and zucchini lengthwise into 2½-in.-thick slices. Wash peppers, remove stems and seeds, and cut into 4 uniform pieces. The mushrooms and onions will be grilled whole. Brush summer squash, peppers, zucchini, mushrooms, and onions with 2 tbsp. olive oil, and season with sea salt and pepper. Preheat the grill to 500–550°F. Turn down to medium heat, and with the lid down, grill veggies 3–5 minutes on each side or until tender. **Note:** Peppers should be slightly charred when done. Remove from grill, cool, and chop into bite-sized squares.

4: **ASSEMBLE SALAD.** In a large, shallow bowl, combine the tortellini, Basil and Sun-Dried Tomato Vinaigrette, grilled veggies, cheeses, fresh basil, tomatoes, and crumbled pistachios. Gently fold together, and keep cool until ready to serve.

Basil and Sun-Dried Tomato Vinaigrette

½ c. balsamic vinegar

2 tbsp. honey

½ c. fresh basil

4 tbsp. sun-dried tomatoes, minced

1 clove garlic (optional)

1 tsp. sea salt

1 tsp. ground black pepper

1 c. really special green and fruity rich olive oil

Put balsamic vinegar, honey, basil, sun-dried tomatoes, garlic (optional), salt, and pepper into a small blender. Blend together until smooth, and pour into a quart-sized glass bowl. Slowly whisk in the olive oil until emulsified, and set aside until time to assemble salad.

Picnic Table Potato Salad with Stone-Ground Mustard Vinaigrette

THIS POTATO SALAD is perfect for summer picnic gatherings because it's dairy-free—no mayonnaise, no eggs, and no cheese. The Yukon Gold potatoes provide a creamy flavor and a good source of potassium. The tarragon, garlic, and stone-ground mustard give it a crowd-pleasing boost of flavors. This isn't your grandma's potato salad—depending on who your grandma is!

3 lb. Yukon Gold potatoes

½ c. olive oil

½ tsp. sea salt

¼ tsp. ground pepper

½ tsp. dried tarragon

1 c. fresh tarragon (save a sprig for garnish)

1 c. garlic chives (Fresh chives could be used if garlic chives are not available. Save a couple of blossoms for garnish if the chives are blooming.)

Some cracked mixed peppercorns, if desired

1: **PREPARE POTATOES.** Scrub potatoes with skins on, and cut into 1½-in. chunks. Preheat oven to 375°F. In a large bowl, toss potatoes with olive oil, salt, pepper, and dried tarragon. Spread out onto a baking sheet, and roast in oven for about 50 minutes. Remove from oven, and cool.

2: **PREPARE VINAIGRETTE.**

3: **PREPARE HERBS**. Rinse, gently pat dry, and chop the tarragon and garlic chives (or regular fresh chives). Save a sprig of tarragon for garnish.

4: **ASSEMBLE SALAD.** When potatoes are cool, place them into a large, shallow serving bowl. Add the chopped chives and fresh tarragon, and pour in the Stone-Ground Mustard Vinaigrette, distributing evenly. Toss gently to combine; garnish with a chive blossom or a fresh sprig of tarragon. This can be served at room temperature and is safe to sit out on the picnic table or on a buffet without refrigeration for a few hours.

Stone-Ground Mustard Vinaigrette

8 tbsp. balsamic vinegar

4 tbsp. honey

2 tsp. stone-ground mustard (coarsely ground)

2 tsp. sea salt

1 tsp. ground black pepper

1 c. olive oil

Place balsamic vinegar, honey, mustard, sea salt, and pepper into a small blender. Blend ingredients together to completely combine. Pour into a bowl, and slowly whisk in the olive oil until thoroughly combined. Pour into a glass jar, cover, and set aside until potatoes are cool enough to toss.

Tri-Color Marinated Pole Bean Salad with Lemon and Chive Vinaigrette

SERVES 6–8

THIS SALAD CAPITALIZES on the many different colors of "green" beans sold at farmers' markets. One purple variety of green bean is called purple podded, and it's a pole bean. There are also yellow green beans, including Beurre de Rocquencourt, a variety of French heirloom beans. Cook by steaming or blanching until they are tender and crisp.

- 7 oz. baby mixed red and green oak lettuce leaves
- ⅓ lb. purple podded pole beans
- ⅓ lb. green pole beans
- ⅓ lb. yellow wax beans
- 2 hard-boiled egg yolks (to grate as garnish)
- 1 c. PastureLand Dairy Thoten cheese (a young parmesan cheese)
- 1 c. roasted almonds (see recipe on page 13)
- Cracked pepper

1: **PREPARE VINAIGRETTE.**

2: **PREPARE PRODUCE.** Wash and thoroughly dry the greens. To blanch beans, bring 1 in. of water to a boil in a large pot fitted with a steamer basket. Place washed beans, stem ends trimmed, into the steaming basket. Cover and steam until crisp and tender, 5–8 minutes. Immediately plunge beans into ice water. Swish around until completely cool. Dry thoroughly by patting with a clean kitchen towel. Put beans in a shallow dish, pour marinade over beans, and toss carefully. Put in refrigerator until salad assembly. This can be prepared a day beforehand.

3: **ASSEMBLE SALAD.** Arrange greens on salad plate or platter, remove beans from vinaigrette, and add the remaining vinaigrette to the reserved vinaigrette. Mound the beans by alternating colors in a pretty row on top of the greens. Grate hard-boiled egg yolks over beans and greens; sprinkle with grated cheese, almonds, and fresh-cracked pepper. Just before serving, drizzle Lemon and Chive Vinaigrette over whole salad, and pour extra vinaigrette into a little pitcher on the side.

Lemon and Chive Vinaigrette

- 8 tbsp. fresh Meyer lemon juice
- 2 tbsp. local honey
- 2 tsp. Dijon mustard
- 2 tbsp. fresh chives, chopped
- 2 tsp. sea salt
- ½ tsp. ground black pepper
- 1 c. olive oil
- ½ tbsp. lemon zest

Put lemon juice, honey, mustard, chives, salt, and ground pepper into blender, and blend together until smooth. Pour into a bowl, and slowly whisk in the olive oil and ½ tbsp. lemon zest. Blend until emulsified (completely combined), and set aside.

Farmers' Market Cobb Salad
with Buttermilk and Peppercorn Dressing

THIS RECIPE HIGHLIGHTS many wonderful fresh vegetables available at the farmers' markets during the summer, along with a superior blue-veined cheese—the Amablu Gorgonzola Cheese.

4 thick slices grainy whole-wheat bread
½ c. extra-virgin olive oil
1 tsp. dried basil
1 tsp. dried oregano
½ c. roasted sunflower seeds (see page 13)
7 oz. mixed greens
1 lb. green beans
2 c. garden cherry tomatoes (red and yellow)
4 baby carrots with green leaves still attached
½ c. red onion
2 c. fresh, raw sweet corn
4 chicken breasts, grilled and cut into 1-in. cubes
2 c. hickory-smoked bacon, cooked crisp
4 hard-boiled eggs, cut in fourths
4 Chioggia beets, roasted and peeled
1 c. Amablu Gorgonzola Cheese, crumbled

1: **PREPARE DRESSING.**

2: **PREPARE CROUTONS.** Keep oven at 275°F. Cut bread into ¼-in. squares, and put squares in a big glass bowl. Toss with ½ c. extra-virgin olive oil, dried basil, and dried oregano. Spread out onto a cookie sheet, and toast along with the sunflower seeds for 20–25 minutes until golden and crunchy. Let cool.

3: **PREPARE PRODUCE.** Wash and thoroughly dry the mixed greens, then tear into bite-sized pieces. Wash the green beans, cherry tomatoes, and baby carrots. Remove the tips from the green beans, blanch, and let cool. Cut the cherry tomatoes in half and the

baby carrots into fourths lengthwise. Dice the red onion in larger pieces, and cut the raw sweet corn off the cobs.

4: **ASSEMBLE SALAD.** Divide and arrange greens on 8 pretty dinner-sized plates. Divide evenly and arrange chicken, bacon, eggs, tomatoes, carrots, green beans, Chioggia beets, and cheese neatly on top of the lettuce. Decorate each salad with croutons, and sprinkle with sunflower seeds. Just before serving, drizzle each salad with Creamy Buttermilk and Peppercorn Dressing.

Buttermilk and Peppercorn Dressing

2 tbsp. rice vinegar	1 tsp. sea salt
1 tsp. Dijon mustard	½ tsp. green
¼ c. olive oil	peppercorns
2 tbsp. honey	1½ c. olive oil–based
2 tbsp. scallions,	mayonnaise
chopped (green ends)	¼ c. buttermilk

Put vinegar, mustard, oil, honey, fresh scallions, sea salt, and green peppercorns into a small blender. Blend together until smooth. Pour into a glass bowl, and slowly whisk in the mayonnaise and buttermilk until creamy smooth. Pour into a glass jar and refrigerate until ready to use.

Asian Summer Slaw with Honey Ginger Vinaigrette

SERVES 6–8

THIS SUMMERTIME SLAW features unique Elephant Heart plums, which are distinctively heart-shaped with skin that is dark reddish-crimson and mottled. The rich, firm flesh of this Japanese variety is blood red and very juicy. These sweet yet tart plums are clingstone fruits, meaning that their flesh clings to the pit. For fun, serve this salad in Asian teacups.

8 hot pink or crimson-colored fleshed plums
(Elephant Heart plums, Santa Rosa plums, or instead try pluots, a complex cross-hybrid of a plum and apricot)

½ head red cabbage

½ head green cabbage

½ c. scallion greens, chopped

⅛ c. toasted black sesame seeds

1: **PREPARE VINAIGRETTE.**

2: **PREPARE PLUMS.** After gently washing, lay plum down on its side, seam facing you, and stem at 12:00 on a cutting board. With a very sharp paring knife and one hand holding the fruit steady, cut both sides of the fruit clean off the stone (pit) in the middle. Next, cut remaining fruit off the stone, and discard the stone. Lay slices of plum facedown on a cutting board, and cut into 8–10 clean and uniform wedges. Set aside until ready to assemble salad.

3: **PREPARE PRODUCE.** Wash the red and green cabbage, thoroughly dry, and cut into 1x⅛-in. julienne bite-sized pieces. Rinse the scallion greens, and finely slice diagonally.

4: **ASSEMBLE SALAD.** In a large glass mixing bowl, add all salad ingredients together except plums. Add Honey Ginger Vinaigrette and gently toss ingredients together to distribute sesame seeds and scallion greens. Be sure to cover all the cabbage with vinaigrette. Keep cool, and just before serving, gently fold in fresh plum wedges, being careful not to damage or break them.

Honey Ginger Vinaigrette

¼ c. rice vinegar

4 tbsp. local honey

1 tbsp. fresh ginger, skin removed

½ clove fresh shallot, cut in small pieces

⅛ tsp. sesame oil

1 tsp. sea salt

½ tsp. ground black pepper

½ c. olive oil

Put vinegar, honey, ginger, shallot, sesame oil, sea salt, and pepper into a small blender. Blend ingredients together until smooth. Pour these ingredients into a glass bowl, and slowly whisk in the olive oil (be careful not to whisk too much) until smooth and emulsified. Pour into a small glass jar, and set aside in cool place until ready to use.

Old-School Potato Salad
with Creamy Turmeric Dressing

SERVES 14–16

WANT A TRADITIONAL potato salad with some flair? The turmeric in this recipe provides just that. Turmeric is a root that looks very much like ginger root except that it's bright orange on the inside. Turmeric has a sharp, slightly bitter flavor and is most commonly used in dried, powdered form. The root is widely cultivated in India and the Caribbean. Enjoy this great potato salad at a cookout!

8 hard-boiled eggs (Reserve 1 egg to cut in wedges for garnish.)

16 medium red potatoes

2 c. celery stalks, chopped

1 c. sweet Vidalia onion, chopped

½ c. dill pickles

½ c. fresh parsley

2 c. sweet red bell pepper, chopped

1: **PREPARE DRESSING.**

2: **PREPARE EGGS.** Hard-boil the eggs and slice. Reserve 1 egg to cut into wedges for garnish.

3: **PREPARE PRODUCE.** Wash the potatoes with skin on, boil until tender throughout but still firm, and cool. Cut into 1½-in. cubes. Wash and chop the celery, saving the ends and leaves for soup stock. Chop the onion, and finely chop the pickles and rinsed parsley. Wash peppers, take the seeds out, and chop.

4: **ASSEMBLE SALAD.** Fold into the large glass bowl of dressing all of the salad ingredients, starting with the chopped dill pickles, parsley, onions, red bell pepper, celery, eggs, and finally the potatoes. Toss all the ingredients together to cover everything with dressing, being careful not to smash the potatoes. Add more of the dressing if it seems too dry. It should be very creamy and saturated with dressing. Garnish with reserved hard-boiled egg and dill weed. Keep salad cool until ready to serve.

Creamy Turmeric Dressing

4 tbsp. rice vinegar

¼ c. dill pickle juice

6 tbsp. honey

3 tbsp. red onion, chopped

4 tbsp. Dijon mustard

1 tbsp. turmeric

4 tsp. sea salt

2 tsp. ground black pepper

2 c. olive oil–based mayonnaise

1 c. sour cream

2 tbsp. fresh dill, chopped fine

(Reserve one sprig of dill for garnish.)

In small blender, combine rice vinegar, pickle juice, honey, onion, Dijon mustard, turmeric, sea salt, and pepper until blended. Pour into a 4-qt. glass bowl, and slowly whisk in mayonnaise, sour cream, and fresh dill. Whisk gently to combine well, and spoon half this dressing into another small bowl. Set small bowl aside.

Sweet Corn and Confetti Cabbage Slaw with Creamy Cilantro and Cayenne Pepper Dressing

THERE'S NOTHING LIKE fresh, local sweet corn in the summertime! Buy enough to serve it on the cob with one meal, and then save a couple of raw ears for the next day to make this healthy, spicy slaw.

¼ c. fresh cilantro

1 whole sweet red bell pepper

2 c. fresh, raw sweet corn

16 oz. red and green cabbage, chopped confetti style

½ c. roasted pistachios (see recipe on page 13)

1: **PREPARE DRESSING.**

2: **PREPARE PRODUCE.** Rinse, gently pat dry, and chop the cilantro into small pieces. Wash and remove the seeds from the bell pepper and then chop confetti style. Rinse the sweet corn after removing the husk and silk, and cut the raw corn off the cob.

3: **ASSEMBLE SALAD.** Put all salad ingredients into 2-qt. glass bowl, and fold in Creamy Cilantro and Cayenne Pepper Dressing. Combine well, and serve right away.

Creamy Cilantro and Cayenne Pepper Dressing

¼ c. rice vinegar

6 tbsp. honey

4 tbsp. red onion

½ tsp. garlic powder

1 tbsp. fresh cilantro, chopped

⅛ tsp. cayenne pepper

1 tsp. sea salt

½ tsp. ground black pepper

½ c. heavy whipping cream

1 c. olive oil–based mayonnaise

½ c. olive oil

1 c. SarVecchio Parmesan cheese, grated (or a comparable local Parmesan)

Put vinegar, honey, onion, garlic, cilantro, cayenne, salt, and pepper into a small blender. Whirl until combined and smooth. Pour into glass mixing bowl, and gently whisk in cream, mayonnaise, olive oil, and cheese to combine. Set aside, and keep cool.

Apricot and Arugula Salad
with Curried Apricot Vinaigrette

SWEET JUICINESS with a bit of tanginess—what more could you ask for on a warm summer day? Apricots, relatives of the peach, provide an abundance of flavor and good nutrition including vitamin A, potassium, magnesium, and iron. Apricots have a velvety soft skin that varies in color from pale yellow to deep orange with a light pink blush. The flesh will range from a golden cream to a brilliant orange. The unique blending of flavors with the apricots, arugula, and cashews in this recipe contrasts nicely with the spice of the curry in the vinaigrette.

8 golden apricots

7 oz. fresh arugula

½ c. scallions

1 c. roasted pistachios (see page 13)

1: **PREPARE VINAIGRETTE.**

2: **PREPARE APRICOTS.** Wash and dry fruit, then, with a sharp knife, cut a slab of fresh fruit off each side of the pit (also called the stone) of the fruit. Flip the fruit, and cut the smaller sides of the fruit off the pit also. Lay the two large slabs facedown on a cutting board, and cut into 4 uniform, thin slices. Cut the smaller slabs to match.

3: **PREPARE PRODUCE.** Wash and thoroughly dry the arugula. Rinse the scallions and julienne-cut them.

4: **ASSEMBLE SALAD.** Arrange arugula on a pretty platter and decorate with cashews, apricots, and scallions. Just before serving, drizzle the salad with Curried Apricot Vinaigrette.

Keep It Fresh

Look for apricots grown closest to your home. Select those that are plump and reasonably firm with a uniform color. Squeeze gently. A ripe apricot will give slightly but should not be too soft. A ripe apricot will be fragrant. Refrigerate up to 3–5 days.

Curried Apricot Vinaigrette

¼ c. rice vinegar

½ tbsp. sweet, not spicy, curry powder (such as Penzey's Sweet Curry Powder)

3 tbsp. apricot preserves (or see page 13)

1 tsp. sweet onion, minced

1 tsp. Dijon mustard

1½ tsp. sea salt

½ tsp. pepper

½ c. fruity green olive oil

Place all vinaigrette ingredients except for olive oil in a small blender. Blend together until smooth and completely blended. Pour into a 1-qt. glass bowl, and gently whisk in the olive oil until combined. Pour dressing into a glass jar, and set aside until ready to assemble salad.

Aunt Nan's Nectarine Salad with Warm Bacon and Nectarine Dressing

SERVES 8

AUNT NAN AND Uncle Paul have always had the most beautiful and bountiful kitchen garden, which supplied and inspired them with fresh and interesting salads. Hosting lunch one summer day, Aunt Nan poured a mixture of sugar, vinegar, and garden onions sautéed in hot bacon grease over fresh garden greens. She called it her "famous wilted greens salad." Recreating Aunt Nan's recipe was a challenge, as memories seem to take on a flavor all their own, but this rendition is close to the original and has Aunt Nan's seal of approval.

8 slices thick-cut hickory-smoked bacon, nitrate free, if available

7 oz. fresh garden green and red leaf lettuces

4 large ripe nectarines

½ c. roasted sunflower seeds (see page 13)

1 peapod for garnish

1: **COOK BACON.** In a medium skillet, cook bacon over medium heat. Toss occasionally until browned, 6–8 minutes. Turn off burner, and with a slotted spoon, transfer bacon to a towel-lined plate to drain. Set bacon aside to cool. Let bacon grease cool and then pour into a glass dish or bowl, keeping 3 tbsp. drippings in the skillet for the dressing. After bacon has cooled, snip 8 slices diagonally into ¼-in. pieces. Crumble the other slice of bacon to use for the Warm Bacon and Nectarine Dressing.

2: **PREPARE DRESSING.**

3: **PREPARE PRODUCE.** Wash and thoroughly dry the greens and nectarines. With a sharp knife, cut a piece of fresh fruit off each side of nectarine pit (the stone of the fruit). Flip fruit, and cut the smaller sides of the fruit off the pit too. Cut the fruit into 1-in. cubes.

4: **ASSEMBLE SALADS.** While dressing is cooling, divide garden greens onto 8 pretty salad plates. Decorate with nectarines, sprinkle with snipped bacon, and spoon 2 tbsp. Warm Bacon and Nectarine Dressing over each salad. Sprinkle with sunflower seeds, garnish with peapod, and serve immediately.

Warm Bacon and Nectarine Dressing

3 tbsp. bacon drippings
½ c. fruity green olive oil
½ c. chopped scallions
4 tbsp. nectarine, peach, or apricot preserves
¼ c. rice vinegar
1 tsp. Dijon mustard
1 tsp. sea salt
½ tsp. ground black pepper
1 strip bacon

Heat skillet with drippings to low, and carefully whisk in olive oil. Add scallions and cook for 30 seconds. Whisk in nectarine syrup, vinegar, Dijon mustard, salt, pepper, and crumbled bacon. Scrape up browned bits until dressing is well combined. Cool about 10 minutes, so it will be safe to spoon over plated salads.

Rainier Cherry Salad
with Cherry Vinaigrette

RAINIER CHERRIES, created in 1952 at Washington State University by Harold Fogle and named in honor of Mount Rainier, are a cross between Bing and Van cherries. They boast a super sweet-tart flavor and provide an excellent source of antioxidants. They are considered a premium variety of cherry and are delicious in this salad.

7 oz. mixed baby greens

1 lb. fresh and ripe Rainier cherries

1½ c. chèvre, crumbled (If you choose a log or cake of chèvre, freeze it until it is firm and then crumble it)

1½ c. roasted walnuts (see recipe on page 13)

1: **PREPARE VINAIGRETTE.**

2: **PREPARE PRODUCE.** Wash and thoroughly dry the mixed baby greens. Wash and dry the cherries, remove the pits, and cut into halves.

3: **ASSEMBLE SALAD.** Arrange greens on a pretty platter or on salad plates. Decorate with chèvre, walnuts, and cherries. Just before serving, drizzle with Cherry Vinaigrette.

Keep It Fresh

When shopping, buy organic cherries with their stems intact, as cutting off cherry stems causes this fragile fruit to quickly deteriorate. Due to high sugar content, Rainier cherries usually have some skin discoloration, brown spotting, or slight scuffing. Look for cherries that are not bruised, splitting, or shriveled. Refrigerate your cherries unwashed in a plastic bag to preserve freshness. When you use your cherries, take them out of the refrigerator with enough time to wash them and let them come to room temperature. This will help to bring out the full, delicious flavor of your cherries.

Cherry Vinaigrette

¼ c. rice vinegar

3 tbsp. cherry preserves (or see page 13 for a whole-fruit syrup recipe)

1 tbsp. sweet Vidalia onion

1 tsp. sea salt

½ tsp. ground black pepper

½ c. olive oil

Put vinegar, cherry preserves, onion, sea salt, and pepper into small blender. Blend ingredients together until smooth, and pour these ingredients into a glass bowl. Slowly whisk in the olive oil (be careful not to whisk too much) until smooth and emulsified. Pour into a glass jar, and set aside in a cool place until ready to use.

Watermelon and Hidden Springs Feta Salad with Watermelon and Lemon Basil Vinaigrette

SERVES 8

IT WOULDN'T BE SUMMER without trying this refreshingly delightful salad! Because there are numerous varieties of watermelon grown in the United States, make sure you purchase one with seeds for this recipe so you don't miss out on the crunchy goodness of the roasted watermelon seeds.

6 lb. watermelon, cold (reserve seeds for roasting)

½–1 c. watermelon seeds

½ tsp. olive oil (optional)

⅛ tsp. sea salt

7 oz. mixed baby greens

½ c. lemon basil

1½ c. Hidden Springs Farmstead Feta Cheese, crumbled (If Hidden Springs is not available, consult your cheesemonger for a local feta cheese.)

1: **PREPARE THE WATERMELON.** Wash the rind of the watermelon with regular soap or with a vegetable wash. Slice into as many 1-in.-thick wedges as you can. Cut the rind off each wedge with a paring knife tip, and cut each wedge into 1-in. rows. Cut the rows into 1-in. cubes. Gently pop out the watermelon seeds as you go along, and set aside for roasting. Place the cubes into a colander, and place a bowl beneath the colander to catch ¼ c. of watermelon juice for the vinaigrette.

2: **PREPARE WATERMELON SEEDS.** Rinse seeds thoroughly in colander and spread out on a cookie sheet to dry. Seeds can be patted dry but roast much better when they are completely dry. Preheat oven to 275°F. Place seeds in a mixing bowl. Add ½ tsp. olive oil (omit if you prefer dry-roasted seeds) and ⅛ tsp. sea salt. Toss together, and spread out on shallow baking pan. Roast 50–60 minutes, until seeds are fragrant and lightly browned. Low and slow is the key to successful roasting. Set aside to cool.

3: **PREPARE VINAIGRETTE.**

4: **PREPARE PRODUCE.** Wash and thoroughly dry the greens. Rinse lemon basil, gently pat dry, and cut chiffonade.

5: **ASSEMBLE SALAD.** Divide baby greens onto 8 pretty summer salad plates, arrange cubes of watermelon on greens, sprinkle with grated cheese and roasted watermelon seeds. Just before serving, drizzle with Watermelon and Lemon Basil Vinaigrette.

Watermelon and Lemon Basil Vinaigrette

6 tbsp. rice vinegar

2 tbsp. honey

¼ c. watermelon juice

1 tbsp. fresh lemon basil

1 tsp. Dijon mustard

1 tsp. sea salt

½ tsp. fine-ground black pepper

½ c. light golden olive oil

Place vinegar, honey, watermelon juice, lemon basil, mustard, salt, and ground pepper into a small blender and blend to combine. Pour into a bowl, and slowly whisk in the olive oil. Store in a glass jar, cover, and keep cool.

Autumn Salads

FOR ME, there is no more glorious time of year than autumn. The pantry shelves are lined with pretty jars of preserved whole-fruit syrups, jams, jellies, and tomatoes, just waiting to add a burst of flavor to handcrafted vinaigrettes. The farmers' markets are loaded with every type of vegetable imaginable, from eggplant to brussels sprouts to endive.

In the fall, I love to visit the local apple orchard to taste heirloom varieties against the new breeds. I take time every autumn to reconnect with family and friends. After sharing a wonderful meal, there is nothing better than a long walk on roads canopied with leaves in an explosion of color. This is the perfect time to remember my grateful list, to relax and be mindful of the season's beauty.

Sweet Seckel Pear and Dried Wild Blueberries Salad with Savory Blueberry Vinaigrette

SERVES 8

USE PERFECTLY RIPE pears in this salad for best flavor. When ripe, Seckel pears have a pleasant yellow hue and will yield to gentle pressure at the stem end of the fruit.

8 slices honey wheat bread

1 tbsp. olive oil

3 oz. Bent River Camembert cheese

24 fresh sprigs fresh thyme

1 c. dried organic wild blueberries

7 oz. mixed green leaf lettuce

4 ripe but firm Seckel pears

1½ c. walnuts

1: **PREPARE CROSTINI.** Preheat oven to 270°F. Using parchment or tracing paper, trace the pear leaf on this page, and cut it out. Next, trace the leaf design onto a thicker piece of construction paper, and cut it out. Use this as a template to cut the bread into pear leaf shapes with a clean sharp paring knife or kitchen scissors. Cut out 16 leaves (approximately 2 leaves per slice of bread), brush both sides with olive oil, and toast in the oven for 20–25 minutes. Remove from oven, and cool completely. When cool, use a small butter knife to spread ½ tsp. camembert on each little leaf. Decorate with sprigs of thyme and a dried blueberry or two. Set in a cool, dry place until ready to assemble salad.

2: **PREPARE VINAIGRETTE** following instructions on page 44.

3: **PREPARE PRODUCE.** Wash and thoroughly dry the greens. Rinse and gently pat dry the thyme. Wash pears and cut each pear into 8 slices. This will provide 4 slices per salad.

4: **ASSEMBLE SALAD.** Divide greens, and arrange on 8 pretty salad plates. Fan 4 pear slices per salad over the greens, sprinkle with walnuts and dried blueberries, and arrange the crostini at the top of the fanned pear. Just before serving, drizzle salads with Savory Blueberry Vinaigrette.

CROUTON TEMPLATE

Autumn Dried Apricot and Couscous Salad with Curried Apricot Vinaigrette

SERVES 8

TECHNICALLY NOT A GRAIN or a pasta, couscous is granular semolina (the hard cracked wheat produced in the milling process by the first crushing) that is moistened and rolled in flour. It is a staple of North Africa and parts of the Middle East. The couscous and pecans in this recipe provide great texture and substance. When apricots, currants, and curry are added into the mix, the result is a savory, spicy comfort food welcome on chilly autumn days.

2½ c. water
2 c. couscous
½ tsp. salt
1 tbsp. olive oil
1 c. scallions, chopped
1½ c. dried apricots (sulfur free)
½ c. dried currants
1½ c. roasted pecans (see recipe on page 13)

Curried Apricot Vinaigrette

¼ c. rice vinegar
½ tbsp. sweet, not spicy, curry powder (such as Penzey's Sweet Curry Powder)
3 tbsp. apricot preserves (or apricot whole fruit syrup from page 13)

1 tsp. sweet onion, minced
1 tsp. Dijon mustard
1½ tsp. sea salt
½ tsp. ground black pepper
½ c. fruity green olive oil

Place all dressing ingredients except for olive oil in kitchen blender or small food processor. Blend together until smooth and completely blended, pour into 1-qt. glass bowl, and gently whisk in olive oil until combined. Pour dressing into glass jar, and set aside until ready to assemble salad.

1: **PREPARE COUSCOUS.** Put water into a 2-qt. saucepan, bring water to a boil, and add couscous and salt. Stir to combine, remove pan from heat, and let couscous stand, covered, for 5 minutes. Fluff couscous with a fork, and transfer to a large glass bowl. Stir in 1 tbsp. olive oil, and cool completely, stirring occasionally.

2: **PREPARE DRESSING.**

3: **PREPARE PRODUCE.** Rinse scallions and chop. Cut dried apricots julienne.

4: **ASSEMBLE SALAD.** Combine all the salad ingredients into the bowl with the couscous. Fold in 1 c. of the Curried Apricot Vinaigrette, and gently toss all together. Add more vinaigrette if necessary, or serve on the side in a little pitcher.

Persimmon and Spicy Pumpkin Seed Salad with Chili Cranberry Vinaigrette

FUYU PERSIMMONS add wonderful color and superb flavors to this salad. With its red-orange skin and flesh, the Fuyu persimmon resembles a tomato, but it tastes like a blend of papaya and mango with a hint of apricot. Persimmons provide a good source of vitamin A and vitamin C.

2 c. pepitas (pumpkin seeds)
⅛ tsp. olive oil
⅛ tsp. sea salt
⅛ tsp. chili powder
7 oz. arugula
4 ripe Fuyu persimmons
½ c. Farmdog Raw Milk Blue Cheese, crumbled
½ c. dried cranberries

1: **PREPARE PUMPKIN SEEDS.** Preheat oven to 275°F. Place seeds in mixing bowl, and add ⅛ tsp. olive oil, ⅛ tsp. sea salt, and ½ tsp. chili powder. Toss together, and spread out on a shallow baking pan. Roast 30–40 minutes, until nuts are fragrant and lightly browned. Low and slow is the key to success for roasting nuts and seeds.

2: **PREPARE VINAIGRETTE.**

3: **PREPARE PRODUCE.** Wash and dry the arugula. Wash the persimmons gently in cool water, trim off the tops, remove cores if necessary, and slice into wedges.

4: **ASSEMBLE SALAD.** Arrange arugula on a pretty serving platter or in a large shallow bowl. Sprinkle with grated blue cheese, decorate with persimmons, and sprinkle with dried cranberries and spicy pepitas. Just before serving, drizzle with Chili Cranberry Vinaigrette.

Chili Cranberry Vinaigrette

3 tbsp. frozen cranberry juice concentrate
¼ c. rice vinegar
1 tsp. chili powder
1 tsp. sweet onion, minced
1 tsp. stone-ground mustard
1 tsp. sea salt
½ tsp. ground black pepper
½ c. light golden buttery olive oil

Place all vinaigrette ingredients except for olive oil in a small blender and blend until smooth. Pour into 1-qt. glass bowl, and slowly whisk in the olive oil. Pour into a glass jar or little pitcher, and keep cool until ready to serve.

Keep it fresh

Select persimmons that are brightly colored, smooth, and glossy. They should be plump and soft (not mushy). However, the Fuyu variety should be quite firm. Unripe persimmons may be put in a paper bag and kept at room temperature for 1–2 days. Once they are ripe, refrigerate your persimmons in a plastic bag for 3–5 days.

Mediterranean Roasted Beet Salad with Fennel and Sweet Orange Vinaigrette

FENNEL IS A PERENNIAL herb that has a sweet, licorice flavor. There are two main varieties of fennel: Florence fennel and common fennel. It is the common fennel that provides the greenish-brown, oval fennel seeds used in this recipe. Enjoy the creative combination of taste and textures in this exquisite side salad.

4 golden beets

4 red beets

1 tbsp. olive oil

1 c. wild rice

7 oz. mixed autumn greens (choose from arugula, chicory, curly endive, mustard greens, and romaine)

1 c. Carr Valley Feta cheese, crumbled

½ c. pitted, sun-dried California olives (Santa Barbara Organic Olives are a good choice.)

1½ c. walnuts, crumbled fine

1: **PREPARE BEETS.** Preheat the oven to 350°F. Wash the beets thoroughly, remove greens (save for another recipe), and leave the skins on. Place beets in a small roasting pan lined with foil. Toss with 1 tbsp. of olive oil, cover with foil, and roast for 45–60 minutes or until a knife can slide easily through the largest beet. Remove from oven and cool. Peel each beet, wipe clean, and cut into little half moons. Set aside.

2: **PREPARE FENNEL SEEDS.** To toast, put the fennel seeds for the vinaigrette in a dry, heavy skillet over medium heat, stir until fragrant and a shade darker, 3–5 minutes. Set aside to cool.

3: **PREPARE WILD RICE.** Cook wild rice al dente and cool until ready to assemble salad.

4: **PREPARE VINAIGRETTE.**

5: **ASSEMBLE SALAD.** Arrange greens on a large salad platter, and sprinkle with feta and wild rice. Decorate with golden and red roasted beets, olives, and walnuts. Just before serving, drizzle with Fennel and Sweet Orange Vinaigrette.

Fennel and Sweet Orange Vinaigrette

2 tbsp. frozen orange juice concentrate

1 tbsp. toasted fennel seeds

¼ c. fresh-squeezed orange juice

1 tsp. sea salt

½ tsp. fine-ground black pepper

½ tbsp. red onion, chopped

½ c. fruity olive oil

Place all vinaigrette ingredients except for olive oil in a small blender, blend together until smooth and completely blended, and pour into 1-qt. glass bowl. Gently whisk in olive oil, and set aside until ready to assemble salad.

Orchard Apple and Green Kale Chopped Salad with Maple Cream Dressing

CRISP APPLES and the flavor of real maple syrup infuse this salad with the essence of fall. Garnish with a favorite locally made tangy blue cheese, such as St. Pete's Select, and this salad is sure to be a favorite.

7 oz. fresh green kale (2 bunches)

4 fresh-picked local orchard apples

½ c. red onion, chopped

¼ c. fennel bulb, chopped

1½ c. roasted pecans (see page 13)

1 c. St. Pete's Select Blue Cheese, crumbled

½ c. golden unsulfured raisins (optional)

1: **PREPARE DRESSING.**

2: **PREPARE PRODUCE.** Wash and thoroughly dry the produce. Remove the ribs of the kale and chop into bite-sized pieces. Chop the apples into bite-sized pieces. Finely chop the red onion and the fennel bulb.

3: **ASSEMBLE SALAD.** Place all chopped salad ingredients into a large mixing bowl. Just before serving, gently toss all the ingredients together with the Maple Cream Dressing and transfer into a pretty glass serving bowl. Serve immediately and enjoy.

Maple Cream Dressing

¼ c. rice vinegar

2 tbsp. apple juice concentrate

4 tbsp. pure maple syrup

1 tbsp. red onion, minced

1 tsp. sea salt

½ tsp. ground black pepper

½ c. olive oil

¼ c. heavy whipping cream

Put vinegar, apple juice concentrate, maple syrup, onion, sea salt, and pepper into a small blender and blend until smooth. Pour into a glass bowl. Slowly whisk in the olive oil and cream until smooth and emulsified. Pour into a glass jar, and set aside.

A Historic Blue Cheese

St. Pete's Select Blue Cheese is made by the Faribault Dairy in Minnesota (recently purchased by Swiss Valley Farms Cooperative of Iowa). St. Pete's Select Blue Cheese was created in 1936 in the historic sandstone caves the dairy uses to age its premium blue-veined cheeses by Felix Frederickson. It is the first American blue cheese marketed nationally.

Champagne Grape and Endive Salad with Simple Autumn Vinaigrette

THE SLIGHTLY BITTER endive, incredibly sweet champagne grapes, and warm, tangy Manchego-style cheese provide delectable contrasting flavors in this recipe.

3 oz. curly endive

3 oz. mixed autumn greens (Choose from arugula, chicory, mustard greens, and baby romaine.)

8 small clusters of champagne grapes

½ c. Solé GranQueso, grated large (Solé GranQueso is a Manchego-style cheese from Roth Käse in Wisconsin. If it is not available, consult your cheesemonger for a comparable local cheese.)

1 c. walnuts, large crumble

1: **PREPARE VINAIGRETTE.**

2: **PREPARE PRODUCE.** Wash and thoroughly dry all greens. Tear the endive into bite-sized pieces, and mix with the autumn greens. Wash grapes and separate into 8 small clusters with the stems left in place.

3: **ASSEMBLE SALAD.** Divide mixed autumn greens among 8 pretty, autumnal salad plates, sprinkle with cheese and walnuts, and garnish with clusters of grapes. Just before serving, drizzle with Simple Autumn Vinaigrette.

Simple Autumn Vinaigrette

6 tbsp. balsamic vinegar
½ tsp. shallot, chopped
⅛ tsp. dried sage
2 tbsp. honey
2 tsp. stone-ground mustard
1 tsp. sea salt
1 tsp. ground black pepper
½ c. fruity green olive oil

Place balsamic vinegar, shallot, sage, honey, mustard, salt, and pepper into a small blender. Blend to combine, and pour these ingredients into a glass bowl. Slowly whisk in the olive oil until emulsified. Pour into a glass jar, cover, and keep cool until ready to assemble salad.

NaNa's Brown Sugar and Curly Kale Salad with Brown Sugar Vinaigrette

MOM WOULD MAKE a special birthday meal of tiny short ribs with a wonderful pineapple, soy, and ginger barbeque sauce, jo-jo potatoes, and a yummy coleslaw full of apples, celery, and shredded cabbage with a brown sugar dressing. Mom was a great cook. As a grandma, she was known as "NaNa"—hence the title for this recipe. NaNa's cooking had such an impact on my life—a treasured legacy being passed down in our family from generation to generation.

7 oz. curly kale

4 tart orchard apples

1 lb. baby portabella mushrooms

½ c. green onions, chopped (bulb and greens)

2 tbsp. olive oil

1 c. Solé GranQueso cheese, grated large (or comparable local cheese)

1 c. roasted pecans (see recipe on page 13)

Brown Sugar Vinaigrette

4 tbsp. brown sugar
½ c. rice vinegar
2 tbsp. red onion, chopped
1 tsp. stone-ground mustard

1 tsp. sea salt
½ tsp. ground black pepper
½ c. light golden buttery olive oil

Place all vinaigrette ingredients except for olive oil in a small blender and blend until smooth. Pour into 1-qt. glass bowl, and slowly whisk in the olive oil. Pour into a glass jar or little pitcher, and keep cool until ready to serve.

1: **PREPARE PRODUCE.** Wash and thoroughly dry the kale. Trim leaves from the center rib and cut into bite-sized pieces. Wash apples and cut into half-moon slices. Wash baby portabellas and slice into halves. Wash green onions, and chop both bulb and greens. Sauté green onions and mushrooms in 1 tbsp. of olive oil until soft and browned (up to 10 minutes on medium to low heat). Remove from heat, drain, and cool. Sauté the apples until they are soft (2–3 minutes). Remove from heat, drain, and cool.

2: **PREPARE VINAIGRETTE.**

3: **ASSEMBLE SALAD.** Divide and arrange kale on 8 pretty party plates; decorate with sautéed apples, onions, and mushrooms; and sprinkle with grated cheese and pecans. Just before serving, drizzle with Brown Sugar Vinaigrette.

Autumn Cobb Salad
with Cranberry and Sage Vinaigrette

THIS RECIPE TAKES an autumn detour from the traditional Cobb to include Bartlett pears, fresh cranberries, pecans, and smoked blue cheese. The Oregon Blue comes from the Rogue Creamery in Oregon, a creamery dedicated to sustainability.

2 tbsp. fresh salted cream butter, softened

1 c. extra-virgin olive oil

½ tsp. dried sage

4 thick-cut slices boule bread

2 c. hickory-smoked bacon, nitrate free, if available

4 hard-boiled eggs

4 red Bartlett pears

2 c. fresh cranberries

7 oz. mixed hearty greens (romaine or spinach)

2 c. Rogue Creamery Oregon Blue Cheese, grated large

3 c. roast turkey breast cut in julienne strips

2 c. roasted pecans (see recipe on page 13)

1: **PREPARE CROUTONS.** Turn oven down to 250°F. Mix together butter, olive oil, and dried sage. Cut boule bread into 4 thick slices, and spread on butter/oil/sage mixture. Cut slices into ¼-in. squares, spread out onto a cookie sheet, and toast for 20–25 minutes, until golden and crunchy. Set aside and let cool.

2: **PREPARE BACON AND EGGS.** Cook the bacon, cool, and cut in julienne strips. Hard-boil the eggs, cool, and grate large.

3: **PREPARE VINAIGRETTE.**

4: **PREPARE PRODUCE.** Wash and thoroughly dry the greens. Wash pears and cranberries, dry, and cut pears into 8 uniform slices (4 per salad).

5: **ASSEMBLE SALAD.** Divide fresh greens among 8 dinner-sized plates. Arrange sliced pears, blue cheese, bacon, eggs, fresh cranberries, turkey, and pecans on greens. Divide croutons between salads, and put in a pretty cluster in the center of the composed salad. Just before serving, drizzle salads with Cranberry and Sage Vinaigrette.

Cranberry and Sage Vinaigrette

6 tbsp. frozen cranberry juice concentrate

1 c. rice vinegar

2 tsp. fresh sage, chopped

2 tsp. sweet onion

2 tsp. stone-ground mustard

2 tsp. sea salt

1 tsp. ground black pepper

1 c. light golden buttery olive oil

Place all vinaigrette ingredients except for olive oil in a small blender and blend until smooth. Pour into 1-qt. glass bowl, and slowly whisk in the olive oil. Pour into a glass jar or little pitcher, and keep cool until ready to serve.

Asian Pear and Dried Cherry Salad with Gingered Pear Vinaigrette

SERVES 8

EXTREMELY JUICY, crunchy, sweet, and surprisingly firm to the touch, Asian pears range from green to golden yellow in color. They are a good source of vitamin C and taste superb in their starring role in this recipe.

7 oz. mixed baby greens

2 Asian pears, cut in thin slices

1 c. pitted dried cherries

1 c. roasted hazelnuts (see recipe on page 13)

½ c. SarVecchio Parmesan, shaved into ribbons (or comparable local cheese)

1: **PREPARE VINAIGRETTE.**

2: **PREPARE PRODUCE.** Wash and thoroughly dry the greens. Wash and thinly slice the Asian pears.

3: **ASSEMBLE SALAD.** Divide and arrange greens on 8 salad plates. Sprinkle with dried cherries, arrange Asian pear slices in starburst shape in center of greens, sprinkle with hazelnuts, and decorate with ribbons of SarVecchio Parmesan. Just before serving, drizzle with Gingered Pear Vinaigrette.

Gingered Pear Vinaigrette

4 tbsp. frozen pear juice concentrate (or pear whole fruit syrup from page 13)

¼ c. rice vinegar

1 tbsp. fresh ginger, skin removed

⅛ tsp. dried cinnamon powder

½ clove fresh shallot, chopped

1 tsp. sea salt

½ tsp. ground black pepper

½ c. light golden olive oil

Put concentrated pear juice, vinegar, ginger, cinnamon, shallot, sea salt, and pepper into a small blender. Blend ingredients together until smooth, pour into a glass bowl, and slowly whisk in the olive oil. Pour into a small glass jar, and set aside in a cool place until ready to use.

Shopping 4-1-1

When purchasing, select those with a sweet and fairly strong aroma, and remember, unlike other pears, Asian pears will not give to gentle pressure when squeezed. Even when fully ripe, they are very firm. Asian pears will stay fresh for 1–2 weeks at room temperature and up to 3 months when refrigerated.

Succotash Quinoa Salad with Stone-Ground Mustard Vinaigrette

SERVES 6–8

SUCCOTASH **IS AN** Indian word meaning "boiled whole kernels of corn." A favorite dish in the southern United States, succotash typically contains corn, lima beans, and sometimes green and red sweet peppers. This recipe, giving traditional succotash a creative twist, includes quinoa, edamame, scallions, and cilantro. Great nutrition, appealing textures, and exquisite flavors—who could ask for anything more?

2 c. black quinoa

3 c. water

1 c. frozen edamame

2 c. sweet corn (fresh off the cob) or frozen sweet corn

¼ c. fresh cilantro

¼ c. scallions, chopped

1 c. sweet red bell pepper, chopped

Buy It in Bulk

Quinoa is one of those wonderful foods that you can stock up on in autumn and have on hand throughout the winter. Buy in bulk to reduce packaging waste. Store your quinoa in an air-tight container in a cool, dry place for 3–4 weeks. Refrigerating or freezing will keep quinoa fresh longer, 3–6 months.

1: **PREPARE QUINOA.** Rinse 2 c. black quinoa thoroughly and drain. Add 2 c. quinoa to 3 c. water in a saucepan, bring to a boil, reduce heat, and let simmer until all water has evaporated. Fluff with a fork, and cool.

2: **PREPARE VINAIGRETTE** by following recipe on page 72.

3: **PREPARE PRODUCE.** Thaw and drain the edamame and the sweet corn (or cut off the cob if using fresh). Rinse, pat dry, and chop the cilantro. Wash and chop the scallions and the bell pepper.

4: **ASSEMBLE SALAD.** Put all salad ingredients into a large 3-qt. bowl, and toss together with vinaigrette. Set aside until ready to serve.

Grilled Bartlett Pear Salad with Simple Autumn Vinaigrette

SERVES 8

BARTLETT PEARS, with a very sweet, juicy flavor, have the spotlight in this delectable autumn recipe. The natural flavors and sweetness of pears are enhanced by grilling. Unlike most pears, which do not change color as they ripen, Bartlett pears turn from green to yellow when ripe. Enjoy the flavor and texture combinations of this unique salad—the pears, the Zante currants, and the Solé GranQueso cheese.

4 ripe Bartlett pears

salt to season

7 oz. baby Bibb lettuce

⅛ red onion, sliced

2 c. walnuts

½ c. dried Zante currants

½ c. Solé GranQueso cheese, grated large (or comparable local cheese)

1: **PREPARE PEARS.** To preheat the grill before cooking, set all burners on high heat, and close the lid. Heat for 10 minutes or until thermometer registers 500–550°F. Wash pears and slice lengthwise into 6 slices, cutting along the core. Turn down to medium heat, and, with the lid down, grill the pears just until tender, about 2 minutes per side. Remove the pears from the grill. Season the pears lightly with salt, and cool before salad assembly.

2: **PREPARE VINAIGRETTE** following recipe on page 98.

3: **PREPARE PRODUCE.** Wash and thoroughly dry the greens. Cut pears into 6 slices (3 per salad). Remove the skin and slice the red onion into thin rings and then in halves.

4: **ASSEMBLE SALADS.** Divide baby Bibb leaves between 8 plates in little nests, arrange 3 pear slices on leaves, and sprinkle with walnuts, currants, and cheese. Right before serving, drizzle with the Simple Autumn Vinaigrette.

Grill It Right

Before you grill your pears, consider using soy or natural alternatives rather than petroleum-based cleaners on your grill. Do-it-yourself cleaners offer another great option. A barbecue brush and a paste of baking soda and water will do the trick. You may also cut an onion in half, rub it over the heated rack, and brush a little olive oil on to keep food from sticking.

Harvest Tomato Panzanella Salad
with Basil and Sun-Dried Tomato Vinaigrette

PANZANELLA IS A popular summer Italian dish. It typically consists of bread, fresh tomatoes, onions, basil, olive oil, vinegar, and seasonings. Other ingredients have been added and vary quite a bit, including tuna, hard-boiled eggs, lettuce, cucumber, anchovies, and bell peppers. The more traditional recipes used bread soaked in water or bread browned in olive oil. This recipe stays fairly true to traditional panzanella but is made with flavorful croutons seasoned with amazing SarVecchio Basil and Olive Oil Asiago cheese.

2 tbsp. olive oil

2 tbsp. softened sweet cream butter

1 tsp. dried basil

8 slices thick-cut bread (ciabatta, boule, or pain au levain)

¼ c. SarVecchio Basil and Olive Oil Asiago, finely grated for croutons (If not available, ask your cheesemonger for a comparable local herbed asiago cheese.)

8 c. heirloom tomatoes (fresh and properly ripened)

½ c. fresh basil leaves

¼ c. asiago cheese, grated large

1: **PREPARE CROUTONS.** Preheat oven to 250°F. Mix together olive oil, butter, and dried basil. Spread this mixture on bread slices, cut slices into cubes, and brush the dry sides with the olive oil/butter/basil mixture. Place cubes into mixing bowl, and toss with finely grated asiago. Spread out on a baking sheet, and toast 15–20 minutes, until browned and semi-crunchy. Let cool before assembling salad.

2: **PREPARE VINAIGRETTE** by following recipe on page 71.

3: **PREPARE PRODUCE.** Wash tomatoes and cut into ¾-in. cubes. Wash and pat dry the basil leaves and cut chiffonade.

4: **ASSEMBLE SALAD.** Place cubed tomatoes, croutons, and fresh basil into a large glass bowl. Gently toss with Basil and Sun-Dried Tomato Vinaigrette and large-grated asiago cheese. Let stand about 15 minutes before serving.

SarVecchio Basil and Olive Oil Asiago

The Sartori Family Company, www.sartorifoods.com, makes this award-winning cheese that combines the subtle hand-rubbed flavors of basil and olive oil with the distinctive nuttiness of the company's famous handcrafted asiago. It is available free of the growth hormone rBST. If you can't find the SarVecchio Basil and Olive Oil Asiago, ask your cheesemonger for a good, locally made substitute.

Three Orchard Apple Salad
with Simple Autumn Vinaigrette

THERE ARE MANY delicious varieties of apples to choose from for this delightful autumn salad. Make a day of it with your family and visit an apple orchard. To find an orchard, go to www.pickyourown.com. Purchase the varieties listed below, or sample and pick your favorites.

7 oz. baby Bibb or butterhead lettuce leaves

3 apples (Choose 3 different varieties of local orchard apples: Braeburn, Honeycrisp, Granny Smith, Pink Lady, or other favorites you enjoy.)

½ c. raw walnuts, crumbled

1 c. golden raisins

4 oz. smoked cheddar cheese, cut into 16 wedges (Grafton Village Cheese Company Maple Smoked Cheddar from Vermont, Carr Valley Apple Smoked Cheddar Cheese from Wisconsin, or a comparable local smoked cheddar.)

ground black pepper

1: **PREPARE VINAIGRETTE** by following recipe on page 98.

2: **PREPARE PRODUCE.** Wash and thoroughly dry baby Bibb lettuce. If leaves are small (see photo), keep whole. If they are large, tear in half. Wash and dry apples. To avoid browning, slice the apples when you are almost ready to eat. Cut thinly with a sharp knife to have 16 slices from each apple.

3: **ASSEMBLE SALAD.** Choose 8 salad plates, and arrange greens in a little nest on each plate. Arrange the apples (2 slices of each variety) in fanned style on the greens, and sprinkle with walnuts and raisins. Adorn each salad with 2 pieces of the cheddar and a crack of pepper. Just before serving, drizzle with the Simple Autumn Vinaigrette.

Buy It Local

Granny Smith apples are nicely tart and sweet at the same time with a bright green skin and crunchy, juicy texture. **Honeycrisp** apples are yellow-gold blushing red. They have natural shallow dimples that are not signs of deterioration. They are extremely juicy, sweet, and crisp but are more perishable than some other varieties. Enjoy your Honeycrisps while fresh and delicious. **Braeburn** apples provide a sweet-tart, very juicy treat. They vary from golden yellow to green gold to mostly red. **Pink Lady** apples are yellow with a beautiful pink to red blush. They offer a wonderful crispy texture and a superb sweet-tart taste.

Purchase organic apples, as they are ranked number 4 for produce with the highest pesticide load, according to www.foodnews.org.

Kale, Sausage, and Potato Salad with Maple and Hickory-Smoked Bacon Dressing

SERVES 6–8 AS A MAIN DISH

THIS RECIPE FEATURES two great sources of flavor, texture, and nutrition—dinosaur kale (also known as dino kale) and Yukon Gold potatoes. Dino kale is an excellent antioxidant and Yukon Gold potatoes are a good source of potassium, vitamin C, iron, calcium, and protein. This salad makes a hearty main dish and is wonderful served with fresh bread and a plate of fresh fruit and cheese.

4 organic chicken and apple sausages (Applegate Farms brand does not contain nitrates.)

3 oz. fresh dino kale (4–5 whole leaves)

1 c. green onions, chopped

1 c. flat parsley

16–20 baby Yukon Gold potatoes

1: **PREPARE SAUSAGE.** Cook sausage according to package directions, cool, and cut into bite-sized pieces. Put into a large glass bowl.

2: **PREPARE PRODUCE.** Wash kale leaves, thoroughly dry, and with kitchen scissors, cut in bite-sized squares. Wash green onions, dry, and chop fine. Wash flat parsley, gently pat dry, and chop leaves medium. Set aside.

3: **PREPARE POTATOES.** Wash, leaving skins on, and cut baby Yukon Gold potatoes in halves. Boil until cooked through, drain, and put into large glass bowl with cooked sausages. Add the onions and parsley, and toss together.

4: **COOK BACON.** In a medium skillet, cook bacon for dressing over medium heat, tossing occasionally, until browned, 6–8 minutes. With a slotted spoon, transfer to a towel-lined plate to drain. Set bacon aside to cool, and begin dressing.

5: **PREPARE DRESSING.**

6: **ASSEMBLE SALAD.** Add kale to potatoes and fold in the Maple and Hickory-Smoked Bacon Dressing.

Maple and Hickory-Smoked Bacon Dressing

¼ lb. hickory-smoked bacon

3 tbsp. bacon drippings

½ c. fruity green olive oil

½ c. scallions, chopped

¼ c. rice vinegar

4 tbsp. real maple syrup

1 tsp. Dijon mustard

1 tsp. sea salt

½ tsp. ground black pepper

Pour off all but 3 tbsp. drippings from bacon skillet. Return skillet to low heat, and carefully whisk in the olive oil. Add the scallions and cook for ½ minute. Whisk in the vinegar, maple syrup, Dijon mustard, salt, pepper, and crumbled bacon, scraping up browned bits until well combined. Snip the rest of bacon into small pieces and combine with dressing.

Fresh Cranberry and Red Anjou Pear Salad with Cranberry Vinaigrette

TART AND SWEET, cranberries are abundantly harvested in Wisconsin, Massachusetts, Oregon, and Washington, where they grow on trailing vines in large, sandy bogs. This salad would be a perfect, new tradition to begin for Thanksgiving this year!

7 oz. mixed baby greens
36 fresh cranberries
4 ripe red Anjou pears
½ c. Cypress Grove Chèvre, grated
1 c. roasted pecans (see page 13)

1: **PREPARE VINAIGRETTE.**

2: **PREPARE PRODUCE.** Wash and thoroughly dry the mixed baby greens. Wash and dry the cranberries and pears. Cut each of the pears into 8 uniform slices just before assembling the salad.

3: **ASSEMBLE SALAD.** Divide the greens between 8 salad plates. Arrange 4 slices of red Anjou pear upon greens. Sprinkle with chèvre, and decorate with 4 fresh cranberries and the roasted pecans. Just before serving, drizzle with Cranberry Vinaigrette.

Cranberry Vinaigrette

3 tbsp. frozen cranberry juice concentrate
¼ c. rice vinegar
1 tsp. sweet onion, minced
1 tbsp. honey
1 tsp. stone-ground mustard
1 tsp. sea salt
½ tsp. pepper
½ c. light golden buttery olive oil

Place the frozen cranberry concentrate, rice vinegar, sweet onion, honey, mustard, salt, and pepper into a small blender. Blend to combine, and pour into a glass bowl. Slowly whisk in the olive oil until emulsified. Pour into a glass jar, cover, and keep cool until ready to assemble salad.

Keep It Fresh

Pecans are native to America, so make sure to purchase those that are U.S. grown and processed closest to your home. Due to their high fat content, pecans can go rancid. Carefully store pecans in an airtight container for up to 3 months, or freeze for up to 6 months.

Curried Grilled Pork Medallion Salad with Curried Apricot Vinaigrette

SERVES 8

THE COMPLEX FLAVOR of curry powder forms the basis of this delicious salad. Curry powder, a blend of spices, herbs, and seeds including cardamom, chilies, cinnamon, cloves, coriander, cumin, saffron, tamarind, and turmeric comes in two basic styles—standard and "Madras," which is the hotter of the two.

4 lb. pork tenderloin

7 oz. mixed baby autumn greens (Choose from a combination of arugula, chicory, curly endive, kale, mustard greens, baby red and green romaine, and red and green oak leaf.)

½ c. green onion, chopped (for garnish)

½ c. dried apricots

1 c. roasted hazelnuts (see page 13)

1: **PREPARE VINAIGRETTE.**

2: **MARINATE PORK.** Place pork tenderloins into a shallow glass dish, pour half of the vinaigrette over the pork, cover, and refrigerate for at least 1 hour.

3: **GRILL PORK.** Preheat the grill to 500–550°F. Sear pork on direct high heat for 2–4 minutes per side. Turn grill down to medium, and with the lid down, grill tenderloin for 5–6 minutes per side or until meat thermometer reads 155°F for medium (slightly pink inside for perfectly grilled pork). Let meat cool, and cut into ¼-in. thick medallions. Keep in refrigerator until ready to assemble salad.

4: **PREPARE PRODUCE.** Wash and thoroughly dry the mixed greens shortly before salad preparation. Wash green onion and chop for garnish. Snip the apricots into julienne strips with a pair of kitchen scissors.

5: **ASSEMBLE SALAD.** Divide the greens among 8 plates, arrange medallions of pork on the greens, and sprinkle with apricots and hazelnuts. Just before serving, drizzle with Curried Apricot Vinaigrette.

Curried Apricot Vinaigrette

½ c. rice vinegar

1 tbsp. sweet, not spicy, curry powder (such as Penzey's Sweet Curry Powder)

6 tbsp. apricot preserves (or apricot whole fruit syrup recipe on page 13)

2 tsp. sweet onion, minced

2 tsp. Dijon mustard

2½ tsp. sea salt

1 tsp. ground black pepper

1 c. fruity green olive oil

Place all dressing ingredients except for olive oil in a small blender or small food processor. Blend together until smooth and completely blended. Pour into a 1-qt. glass bowl, and gently whisk in olive oil until combined. Use half of the vinaigrette to marinate the pork tenderloins, and set aside the rest until ready to assemble salad.

Dark Cacao-Roasted Sweet Potato Salad with Dark Chocolate and Chili Vinaigrette

SERVES 6–8

THE DELICIOUS FLAVORS of roasted sweet potatoes, yellow pears, almonds, and a hint of cacao make this a unique salad sublime. This salad is guaranteed to brighten and add warmth to the dreariest November day.

4 large sweet potatoes

2 tbsp. olive oil

1 tsp. sea salt

⅛ tsp. fine-ground black pepper

2 tbsp. Dagoba Organic Baking Cacao (fair trade)

7 oz. escarole and endive

2 yellow pears

1 c. roasted almonds (see recipe on page 13)

1: **PREPARE SWEET POTATOES.** Wash and dry sweet potatoes, peel off skins, and cut into ½-in. cubes. Preheat oven to 350°F. In a large mixing bowl, combine sweet potatoes, olive oil, sea salt, and black pepper. Toss together to coat potatoes well. Arrange potatoes in a single layer on a heavyweight, rimmed baking sheet or in a 9x13-in. baking dish. Dust with powdered baking cacao. Place on top rack of oven and roast until tender inside and dark brown on outside, about 60 minutes. Set aside to cool. **Note:** This can be prepared the night before if you prefer.

2: **PREPARE VINAIGRETTE.**

3: **PREPARE PRODUCE.** Wash and thoroughly dry fresh greens. Tear into large, bite-sized pieces. Wash pears, and cut into uniform bite-sized cubes right before assembling salad.

4: **ASSEMBLE SALAD.** Arrange greens on a large serving platter or in a large, shallow bowl. Decorate with roasted sweet potatoes, pears, and roasted nuts. Just before serving, drizzle with Dark Chocolate and Chili Vinaigrette, and enjoy!

Dark Chocolate and Chili Vinaigrette

¼ c. rice vinegar

3 tbsp. maple syrup

1 tbsp. Dagoba Organic Chocolate Syrup (or 2 tbsp. Dagoba Organic Semisweet Baking Chocolate bar, melted)

1 tsp. chili powder

1 tsp. red onion, minced

1 tsp. Dijon mustard

1 tsp. sea salt

½ tsp. ground black pepper

½ c. light golden buttery olive oil

Put vinegar, maple syrup, chocolate syrup, chili powder, onion, mustard, sea salt, and pepper into a small blender. Blend ingredients together until smooth, and pour into a glass bowl. Slowly whisk in the olive oil until smooth and emulsified. Pour into a glass jar, and set aside in a cool place until ready to assemble the salad.

Brussels Sprout Petal Salad with Lemony Sage Vinaigrette

IF YOU'VE NEVER tried brussels sprouts before, you will be amazed with this salad. Brussels sprouts are part of the crucifer family, which includes cabbage, cauliflower, broccoli, and kale. When shopping, look for Brussels sprouts with bright green, small sprouts with compact heads. Smaller sprouts will be nuttier than their mature, more bitter, counterparts. They will also be more tender.

1½ lb. brussels sprouts (save the leaves, also called petals)

1½ c. Vermont Butter & Cheese Creamery Goat's Milk Feta cheese, grated

1 c. roasted walnuts (see recipe on page 13)

1 tsp. lemon zest (for garnish)

2: **PREPARE VINAIGRETTE.**

3: **PREPARE BRUSSELS SPROUTS.** Rinse sprouts, drain, and discard discolored petals (leaves). Using a small, sharp knife, trim the stem end of each sprout to release a layer of petals, then pull the petals apart, all the way to the center of the sprout. Cut the center portion in half lengthwise. You can use all these parts of the brussels sprouts except the outside petals and the stem. Repeat to separate leaves on remaining sprouts. This is a great job for young chefs!

4: **ASSEMBLE SALAD.** Just before serving, put all salad ingredients into a large glass mixing bowl. Toss the brussels sprout petals with the cheese, walnuts, lemon zest, and Lemony Sage Vinaigrette.

Lemony Sage Vinaigrette

6 tbsp. fresh Meyer lemon juice
1 tbsp. local honey
2 tsp. Dijon mustard
⅛ tsp. ground sage

1 tsp. sea salt
½ tsp. ground black pepper
½ c. olive oil

Pour lemon juice, honey, mustard, sage, salt, and ground pepper into a small blender. Blend together until smooth, and pour into a mixing bowl. Slowly whisk in the olive oil, blend until emulsified (completely combined), and set aside.

Autumn Cabbage and Grape Slaw with Simple Autumn Vinaigrette

THERE ARE THOUSANDS of grape varieties to choose from for this delightful slaw. Pick your favorite varieties or try some new varieties, but purchase U.S.-grown organic grapes, if available. This is one of those recipes you'll be coming back to autumn after autumn. Enjoy!

7 oz. green cabbage (1 small cabbage)

2 c. red seedless grapes
(Flame, Ruby, Red Glove, or Scarlet Royal)

2 c. green seedless grapes
(Princess, Thomson, or Calmeria)

1 c. red onion, sliced

1½ c. whole walnuts

1½ c. SarVecchio Parmesan, grated
(or comparable local cheese)

1 c. golden raisins

Keep It Fresh

Green cabbage is juicy and tender with pale green leaves that are thick and tightly wrapped. Choose cabbage heads that have crisp, shiny outer leaves that are tightly bundled. The cabbage should be heavy for its size and variety. It should also be firm. Avoid those with yellowing leaves or other signs of deterioration, and refrigerate in a plastic bag in the crisper up to a week for optimal freshness.

1: **PREPARE VINAIGRETTE** by following recipe on page 98.

2: **PREPARE PRODUCE.** Wash, thoroughly dry, and chop cabbage julienne style. Wash, dry, and cut grapes in halves. Wash and peel red onion, slice in 8 thin slices (rings), and then cut rings in fourths.

3: **ASSEMBLE SALAD.** Layer the salad ingredients in a large, shallow bowl, ending with grapes, walnuts, and cheese. Just before serving, toss with Simple Autumn Vinaigrette.

Hardwood-Smoked Ham and Arugula Salad with Maple and Hazelnut Vinaigrette

SERVES 6–8

THIS RECIPE CALLS for smoked ham, and I recommend Organic Prairie ham. The company has many wonderful meat and poultry products and great information about the benefits of selecting organic meats at its website, www.organicprairie.coop.

7 oz. baby arugula

2 green Anjou pears

24 oz. Organic Prairie hardwood-smoked ham, cut in julienne strips (If Organic Prairie is not available, select another organic hardwood-smoked ham made closest to your home.)

8 oz. Goodhue Grass-Fed Gouda Cheese, sliced julienne (made by PastureLand Dairy, or use another local Gouda cheese)

1 c. roasted hazelnuts, crumbled fine (see recipe on page 13)

1: **PREPARE PRODUCE.** Wash and thoroughly dry the arugula. Wash the pears, dry, and cut into 12 thin slices per pear.

2: **PREPARE VINAIGRETTE.**

3: **ASSEMBLE SALAD.** Divide and arrange arugula on 8 salad plates. Arrange pear slices (3 per salad), julienned smoked ham, and julienned cheese in neat little stacks. Sprinkle with roasted hazelnuts, and right before serving, drizzle with Maple and Hazelnut Vinaigrette.

Maple and Hazelnut Vinaigrette

¼ c. rice vinegar

2 tbsp. apple juice concentrate

4 tbsp. pure maple syrup

1 tbsp. red onion, minced

1 tsp. sea salt

½ tsp. fine-ground black pepper

½ c. hazelnut oil

Put vinegar, apple juice concentrate, maple syrup, onion, sea salt, and pepper into a small blender. Blend ingredients together until smooth, and pour these ingredients into a glass bowl. Slowly whisk in the oil until smooth and emulsified. Pour into a glass jar, and set aside in a cool place until ready to assemble the salad.

Shopping 4-1-1

When you purchase the ham for this recipe, consider purchasing USDA-certified organic ham that was raised and processed close to your home. Organic ham will be free of antibiotics, arsenic-based drugs, animal byproducts, and growth hormones. For more information on organic foods, go to www.greenerchoices.org.

Autumn Waldorf Salad with
Creamy Honey and Sweet Tarragon Dressing

THE WALDORF SALAD was created by Oscar Tschirky at the Waldorf-Astoria Hotel in New York City in 1893. It traditionally contained apples, celery, and mayonnaise. Later, walnuts and then grapes or raisins were added. Since then, many variations have been enjoyed. The following Waldorf provides an amazing flavor combination of blue cheese in the salad and tarragon in the dressing.

7 oz. of fresh arugula
1 c. fennel bulb, chopped julienne
16 small crab apples
1½ c. Farmdog Raw Milk Blue Cheese, crumbled
2 c. roasted walnuts (see recipe on page 13)

1: **PREPARE DRESSING.**

2: **PREPARE PRODUCE.** Wash and thoroughly dry the arugula. Wash and julienne-chop the fennel bulb. Wash the crab apples, remove the stem, and cut into bite-sized wedges.

3: **ASSEMBLE SALAD.** Arrange half the arugula on a pretty salad platter, sprinkle with half the blue cheese, chopped fennel, apples, and walnuts. Then repeat the layering process. Just before serving, drizzle with Creamy Honey and Sweet Tarragon Dressing.

Creamy Honey and Sweet Tarragon Dressing

1 tbsp. sweet Vidalia onion, minced
¼ c. rice vinegar
¼ c. fresh heavy cream
2 tbsp. honey
2 tbsp. fresh tarragon
1 tsp. sea salt
½ tsp. ground black pepper
1½ c. olive oil–based mayonnaise

Put onion, vinegar, heavy cream, honey, tarragon, sea salt, and black pepper in a small blender, and blend until completely combined. Pour these ingredients into a glass bowl, and slowly whisk in the mayonnaise. Whisk together until well combined. Set aside until ready to assemble salad.

Fresh Mozzarella and Shredded Kale Salad with Basil and Sun-Dried Tomato Vinaigrette

PINE NUTS, of adequate quality and desirable flavor, come from about 28 of 100 recognized species of true pines. The taste and texture of the pine nuts along with the fresh mozzarella and sun-dried tomatoes make this salad a sensational prelude to any autumn dinner.

1 c. pine nuts

½ tsp. olive oil

⅛ tsp. sea salt

7 oz. green and red kale

¼ red onion, sliced

½ lb. fresh button mushrooms

1 tbsp. sun-dried tomatoes

3–6 oz. Crave Brothers Fresh Mozzarella, cut in cubes (If Crave Brothers is not available, ask your cheesemonger for a similar tasting local cheese.)

1: **PREPARE PINE NUTS.** Preheat oven to 275°F. Place nuts in mixing bowl. Add 1/2 tsp. olive oil (omit if you prefer dry-roasted nuts) and 1/8 tsp. sea salt. Toss together, and spread out on shallow baking pan. Roast 15–20 minutes, until nuts are fragrant and lightly browned. Low and slow is the key to successful roasting.

2: **PREPARE VINAIGRETTE** by following recipe on page 71.

3: **PREPARE PRODUCE.** Wash and thoroughly dry the kale leaves. With kitchen scissors, cut the leaf away from its center rib, discard rib (or save for vegetable stock), and snip leaves into bite-sized pieces. Remove the skin from the onion, and cut into fourths. Slice the fourths into very thin slices. Wash and scrub earthy stains off mushrooms, dry, and slice into neat, small uniform slices. Drain and chop the sun-dried tomatoes.

4: **ASSEMBLE SALAD.** Using a large shallow bowl or platter, arrange half of the ingredients on the platter in the following order: kale, red onions, mushrooms, little pieces of mozzarella, pine nuts, sun-dried tomato pieces, and repeat. Just before serving, drizzle with Basil and Sun-Dried Tomato Vinaigrette.

Pine Nuts

When you purchase your pine nuts, look first for those grown and processed in the United States. If unavailable, look for a fair trade brand grown closest to your home. Pine nuts may be purchased in bulk but need to be stored carefully as their high fat content leads to rancidity fairly quickly in comparison to many other nuts. Refrigerate up to 3 months in an airtight container, or freeze up to 9 months.

Winter Salads

A MIDWEST WINTER brings with it the beauty and miracle of snow and the giddy anticipation of gathering with family and friends to enjoy favorite foods of the holiday season. Cinnamon, cumin, cardamom, ginger, allspice, and curry are daily scents in the winter kitchen. Stocking the pantry with dried fruits, seeds, nuts, and grains will make it easy to create beautiful and delicious salads. Along with local root vegetables, nuts, maple syrup, and hand-harvested wild rice, we are lucky that our markets also provide exotic fruits from other parts of the country: dried figs and apricots, glorious citrus fruits, quince, kumquats, and that marvelously, ingenious parcel bursting with flavor, the pomegranate. These winter fruits inspire creativity and variety in healthy salad preparation. Enjoy the season!

Merry Fruit Medley Salad with Zesty Pomegranate Cinnamon Vinaigrette

THIS COLORFUL, DELECTABLE salad combines tasty "super foods" like pomegranate, winter citrus, and cranberries to provide a good nutrient boost during the winter months. Best of all, it makes a beautiful starter salad when entertaining for the holidays!

8 kiwis

4 satsuma oranges

2 pomegranates (for seeds)

4 yellow pears

1 c. fresh cranberries

1: PREPARE VINAIGRETTE.

2: PREPARE PRODUCE. Wash and peel skin from kiwi. Slice into fourths. With a sharp paring knife, peel away the skin from the oranges. Working over a bowl to reserve the juice, cut along both sides of each dividing membrane and lift out sections from the center, and set aside. Put 2 pomegranates into a large colander, and immerse into a deep tub of cool water. Cut the top off each pomegranate, break open each pomegranate, pull apart, and tickle the little seeds out of the white membranes. The seeds will drop to the bottom of the colander, and the white membrane and red peel will float to the top of the water. Remove the colander, drain seeds well, and set aside for use later. Wash and dry pears. Cut into bite-sized pieces. Wash and dry cranberries. Set aside.

3: ASSEMBLE SALAD. Choose 8 festive champagne glasses or a clear salad dish. Divide and stack fruit, alternating varieties and sprinkling pomegranate seeds throughout. Place glasses on a pretty and festive holiday plate, and just before serving, drizzle with Zesty Pomegranate Cinnamon Vinaigrette.

Zesty Pomegranate Cinnamon Vinaigrette

1 medium pomegranate (for ¼ c. fresh pomegranate juice)

6 tbsp. rice vinegar

2 tbsp. local honey

½ tsp. cinnamon

1 tsp. sea salt

1 tsp. ground black pepper

½ c. walnut oil

Cut one pomegranate in half and juice on an orange juicer, removing ¼ c. of juice. Place rice vinegar, pomegranate juice, honey, cinnamon, salt, and pepper into a small blender. Blend to combine, and pour into a glass bowl. Slowly whisk in the walnut oil until emulsified. Pour into a glass jar, cover, and keep cool until ready to assemble salad.

Winter Roasted Root Vegetable Salad with Simple Winter Vinaigrette

THIS HEARTY, SAVORY root vegetable salad features a 100 percent organic cow's milk feta cheese made by Organic Valley, www.organicvalley.coop. If Organic Valley Feta Cheese is not available, ask your cheese monger for a comparable locally made feta cheese.

7 oz. winter greens (a mix of escarole, radicchio, endive, arugula, romaine, and frisée)

4 rutabagas

4 turnips

4 parsnips

4 red beets

16 pearl onions

2 tbsp. olive oil, for roasting

¼ tsp. sea salt

¼ tsp. fine-ground black pepper

1 tbsp. dried sage

1½ c. feta cheese (Organic Valley Feta or a similar local feta cheese)

1 c. black olives, snipped

1½ c. roasted walnuts (see page 13)

1: **PREPARE PRODUCE.** Preheat oven to 425°F. Wash and thoroughly dry fresh winter greens. Set aside. Wash and peel rutabagas, turnips, parsnips, and beets. Cut each of the rutabagas and turnips into 8 cubes (4 per salad), and pat dry. Slice the parsnips into 8 long pieces (4 per salad), and pat dry. Cut beets in half the long way (2 per salad), and pat dry. Wash and peel the pearl onions. Keep whole (2 per salad), and pat dry. Brush all vegetables (except winter greens) with olive oil, then sprinkle with sage, salt, and pepper. Spread out on 2 baking sheets, and

roast for 25–30 minutes until browned and cooked entirely through. Set aside to cool until ready to assemble salad.

2: **PREPARE VINAIGRETTE.**

3: **ASSEMBLE SALAD.** Choose 8 dinner-sized plates, and arrange mixed winter greens on each plate. Divide and arrange roasted vegetables upon greens, and sprinkle with feta cheese, olives, and walnuts. Just before serving, drizzle with Simple Winter Vinaigrette.

Simple Winter Vinaigrette

6 tbsp. balsamic vinegar
½ tsp. shallot, chopped
2 tbsp. maple syrup
2 tsp. Dijon mustard
½ tsp. of dried thyme
½ tsp. dried oregano
1 tsp. sea salt
½ tsp. ground black pepper
½ c. walnut oil

Place balsamic vinegar, shallot, maple syrup, mustard, thyme, oregano, salt, and pepper into a small blender. Blend to combine, and pour into a glass bowl. Slowly whisk in the walnut oil until emulsified, and keep cool until ready to assemble salad.

Arugula and Tangerine Salad
with Tangerine Vinaigrette

SERVES 6–8

TANGERINES ARE the most common type of mandarin found in the United States. They have a rough, thick skin, but looks can be deceiving, as the flesh is incredibly sweet and juicy. This salad is a refreshing, citrusy delight that will boost your energy and lift your midwinter spirits.

8 tangerines
7 oz. arugula
1 c. green onion, chopped
½ c. roasted almonds (see page 13)

1: **PREPARE TANGERINES.** With a sharp paring knife, peel away the skin from the fruit. Working over a bowl to reserve the juice, cut along both sides of each dividing membrane, and lift out sections from center. Set aside tangerines, and measure out at least ¼ c. of reserved juice for the vinaigrette.

2: **PREPARE VINAIGRETTE.**

3: **PREPARE PRODUCE.** Wash and thoroughly dry the arugula. Wash and chop the green onions (the green part only).

4: **ASSEMBLE SALAD.** In a large, shallow bowl, arrange the greens, decorate with tangerines, sprinkle with green onions and almonds, and, just before serving, drizzle with Tangerine Vinaigrette.

Tangerine Vinaigrette

¼ c. fresh-squeezed tangerine juice
¼ tsp. tangerine zest
2 tbsp. rice vinegar
2 tbsp. honey
½ tsp. Dijon mustard
¼ tsp. shallot, chopped
⅛ tsp. sesame oil
1 tsp. sea salt
½ tsp. ground black pepper
1 c. sunflower oil

Pour reserved tangerine juice, tangerine zest, rice vinegar, honey, mustard, shallot, sesame oil, sea salt, and black pepper into a small blender. Blend ingredients together until smooth, and pour into a glass bowl. Slowly whisk in the sunflower oil. Set aside in cool place until ready to assemble salad.

Keep It Fresh

Nuts and seeds may be kept fresh for quite a while. Put a label on your nuts and seeds with the date of purchase to help you stay organized. Almonds may be stored in your refrigerator in an airtight container for up to 6 months. If possible, buy almonds in bulk. When buying in bulk, make sure that the bins are covered and that products are fresh.

Ruby Red and Avocado Green Holiday Salad with Ginger Grapefruit Vinaigrette

GRAPEFRUIT, an excellent source of vitamin C, is a hybrid of a pummelo and a sweet orange. Grapefruit segments will be extra juicy if you remove the fruit from the refrigerator 30 minutes before using and gently roll it on the counter before cutting. Enjoy this recipe with your family or with friends. The beautiful red flesh of the grapefruit and the wonderful green spinach make this a perfect holiday salad.

4 large ruby red grapefruit

7 oz. fresh baby spinach leaves

4 ripe but firm avocados

½ c. roasted cashews (see recipe on page 13)

½ tsp. curly lime zest (garnish)

1: **PREPARE GRAPEFRUIT.** With a sharp paring knife, peel away the skin from the fruit. Working over a bowl to reserve the juice, cut along both sides of each dividing membrane, and lift out sections from the center. Set aside, and measure out at least ¼ c. of reserved juice for the vinaigrette.

2: **PREPARE VINAIGRETTE.**

3: **PREPARE PRODUCE.** Gently wash and thoroughly dry the spinach. Wash and dry the avocados. Score avocado skin along the north–south axis. Gently twist halves apart, and score the halves again north–south. Slice into quarters, pull from pit, peel skin away, and remove the pit. Slice each quarter into 4 thin slices.

4: **ASSEMBLE SALAD.** Divide and arrange spinach on 8 festive salad plates. Fan grapefruit and avocado slices over spinach, sprinkle with cashews, zest with lime, and just before serving, drizzle with Ginger Grapefruit Vinaigrette.

Ginger Grapefruit Vinaigrette

¼ c. fresh-squeezed grapefruit juice

¼ c. rice vinegar

1 tbsp. frozen cranberry juice concentrate

2 tbsp. honey

1 tbsp. fresh ginger, grated

1 tsp. Dijon mustard

½ clove fresh shallot, chopped

⅛ tsp. sesame oil

1 tsp. sea salt

½ tsp. ground black pepper

1 c. sunflower oil

Pour reserved grapefruit juice, vinegar, cranberry juice concentrate, honey, ginger, mustard, shallot, sesame oil, sea salt, and black pepper into a small blender. Blend ingredients together until smooth, and pour into a glass bowl. Slowly whisk in the sunflower oil. Set aside in cool place until ready to assemble salad.

NOTE: This recipe makes a little more than needed, so put the extra into a little glass jar. It will stay fresh up to 2 weeks.

Soiree Salad Sampler
with a Variety of Vinaigrettes

SERVES 20–25 GUESTS (1–2 SALADS EACH OF THE 3 VARIETIES)

WHEN YOU'RE entertaining this holiday season, use an assortment of winter salad ingredients and a variety of festive dressings to create fun little canapé salads that will be perfect for entertaining. To serve, use some pretty glass cake stands and stack them to create the perfect party display for these little buffet salads.

1 medium pomegranate
(for ½ c. pomegranate seeds)

3 oz. fresh watercress

3 oz. arugula

3 oz. mixed baby greens

4 fresh kumquats

1 ruby red grapefruit

½ fresh jicama

½ c. chèvre , crumbled

½ c. roasted hazelnuts (see recipe on page 13)

1 avocado

½ c. SarVecchio Parmesan cheese, grated

½ c. roasted pistachios (see recipe on page 13)

2 small Forelle pears

½ c. St. Pete's Select Blue Cheese, crumbled

½ c. raw walnuts

75 confection cups (25 of three different colors—
red, green, and white perhaps)

1: **PREPARE POMEGRANATE.** Cut the pomegranate open at the crown, put into a large colander, and immerse colander into deep tub of cool water. With both hands, break apart the pomegranate into 2 pieces, and gently pull the seeds apart from the white membrane and the skin by tickling the little red seed arils out of the white membranes. The seeds will sink to the bottom of the colander, and the excess skin and membrane will float to the top of the water. When finished seeding the pomegranate, push aside anything on top of the water, and pull the colander out of the water. Set aside to drain. Sort through and clean up any white skin. These seeds can be put into a small covered container and stored in the refrigerator for up to 2 weeks.

2: **PREPARE OTHER PRODUCE.** Wash and thoroughly dry your greens: the watercress, arugula (trim any long stems), and mixed baby greens. Scrub the kumquats really well; rinse, dry, and slice into thin, uniform rounds and then into halves. Set aside. To prepare the grapefruit, rinse and then peel away the skin from the fruit. Use a sharp paring knife, and work over a bowl to reserve the juice for the vinaigrette (⅛ c.). Cut along both sides of each dividing membrane, and lift out sections from center. Cut each slice of grapefruit into bite-sized segments. Set aside. Wash and dry the jicama. Peel and julienne-slice (matchstick-sized pieces).

continued on page 134

3: PREPARE VINAIGRETTES. Prepare Ginger Grapefruit Vinaigrette by following directions on page 130. Prepare Zesty Pomegranate Cinnamon Vinaigrette by following recipe on page 127, and Simple Winter Vinaigrette by following recipe on page 128.

4: ASSEMBLE SALADS. You will need about 2½x3½ ft. of kitchen counter space to set up an assembly line. Line up ingredients for one salad at a time.

KUMQUAT AND JICAMA SALAD: Using 25 confection cups of one color, place 10 leaves of mixed baby greens loosely in each cup. Decorate with kumquat segment and jicama stick, sprinkle with crumbled chèvre, and place a hazelnut on top. Carefully place little salads on a tray, cover, and place in refrigerator until ready to dress with Simple Winter Vinaigrette and assemble on cake stand.

GRAPEFRUIT, AVOCADO, AND ARUGULA SALAD: Wash and dry avocados. Score avocado skin along the north–south axis, and gently twist the halves apart. Score the halves again north–south, and slice into quarters. Pull avocado from the pit, peel skin away, and remove the pit. Slice each quarter into uniform bite-sized pieces.

Using 25 confection cups of a second color, place 10 leaves of arugula loosely in each cup, decorate with grapefruit segment and avocado piece, and sprinkle with grated parmesan and a pinch of crumbled pistachios. Carefully place cups on a tray, cover, and place in refrigerator until ready to dress with Ginger Grapefruit Vinaigrette and assemble on cake stand.

PEAR AND POMEGRANATE SALAD: Wash and dry pears, and cut into bite-sized pieces. Using 25 confection cups of a third color, put 10 watercress leaves loosely into each cup (see photo). Sprinkle with a pinch of crumbled blue cheese, and decorate with a pear slice, a couple of pomegranate seeds, and a bit of crumbled walnut. Carefully place salads on tray, cover, and place in refrigerator until ready to dress with Zesty Pomegranate Cinnamon Vinaigrette and assemble on cake stand.

6: SERVE SALADS. Dress half of each tray with its vinaigrette, placing the rest of the salads back into the refrigerator. Carefully stack cake stands. Starting on the top and moving to bottom of the stands, fill in rows of each salad so all three salads are available on each tier. Do this part on the buffet table because it is very difficult to transport the cake stand once filled.

Buy It Organic

Always buy organic greens. Lettuce ranks thirteenth, spinach eighth, and kale ninth on the list of produce with the highest pesticide loads, according to the Environmental Working Group. Buying organic or growing your own greens are good options. Greens are easily grown in a shallow container, such as a window box, and many varieties can even grow year-round indoors. Plant more seeds every 6–8 weeks to provide a steady supply of the freshest and most local greens around. Check out www.organicgardening.com for further information.

Roots and Fruits Midwinter Salad with White Grapefruit and Coriander Vinaigrette

SERVES 6–8

ROOT VEGETABLES are an essential staple in winter salads. This recipe takes advantage of turnips, which provide a good boost of vitamin C, and parsnips, a good source of fiber. Enjoy the combination of delicious flavors and delightful textures in this midwinter salad.

4 parsnips

4 turnips

salt

pepper

2 tbsp. olive oil

4 white grapefruits

7 oz. mixed baby greens

1 c. grated San Andreas cheese (or another local pecorino-style cheese)

½ c. roasted hazelnuts (see recipe on page 13)

1: PREPARE PRODUCE FOR ROASTING. Wash, dry, and peel parsnips and turnips. Cut the parsnips in half lengthwise. Cut the turnips into fourths. Preheat oven to 400°F. Brush parsnips and turnips with olive oil and then sprinkle lightly with salt and pepper. Roast in oven for 20–25 minutes, cooked through yet firm and browned. Remove from oven, cool, and slice julienne.

2: PREPARE OTHER PRODUCE. Wash and dry grapefruits. With a sharp paring knife, peel away the skin and pith from the fruit. Working over a bowl to reserve the juice, cut along both sides of each dividing membrane, and lift out sections from the center. Discard seeds, skin, and pit. Cut fruit segments into bite-sized chunks, and place in a strainer over the bowl to continue collecting juices. Wash and thoroughly dry mixed baby greens. Set aside in a cool place until ready to assemble salad.

3: PREPARE VINAIGRETTE.

4: ASSEMBLE SALAD. Arrange mixed baby greens on 8 pretty salad plates or a large salad platter. Decorate greens with roasted root vegetables, cheese, and grapefruit. Sprinkle with hazelnuts, and, just before serving, drizzle with White Grapefruit and Coriander Vinaigrette.

White Grapefruit and Coriander Vinaigrette

¼ c. fresh-squeezed grapefruit juice

¼ c. rice vinegar

2 tbsp. honey

1 tsp. Dijon mustard

½ clove fresh shallot, chopped

⅛ tsp. dried coriander

½ tsp. sea salt

¼ tsp. ground black pepper

½ c. roasted hazelnut oil

Pour reserved grapefruit juice, rice vinegar, honey, Dijon mustard, shallot, coriander, sea salt, and black pepper into a small blender. Blend ingredients together until smooth, and pour into a glass bowl. Slowly whisk in the hazelnut oil, and set aside until ready to assemble salad.

Oh, My Darling Clementine Salad
with Cilantro Vinaigrette

THE CHEESE FEATURED in this salad is the Queso Oaxaca Mexican Mozzarella cheese made by the Mozzarella Company, www.mozzco.com. Based in Texas, the Mozzarella Company makes all of its cheese by hand, following centuries-old recipes. The fabulous mozzarella and the tiny, juicy, aromatic clementines will delight your palate in this tasty winter salad.

½ c. pepitas (pumpkin seeds)
½ tsp. olive oil
⅛ tsp. sea salt
7 oz. green leaf lettuce
1 large jicama
8 clementines
½ c. Queso Oaxaca Mexican Mozzarella
   cheese, grated

1: **PREPARE PUMPKIN SEEDS.** Preheat oven to 275°F. Place seeds in a mixing bowl. Add ½ tsp. olive oil (omit if you prefer dry-roasted seeds) and ⅛ tsp. sea salt. Toss together, and spread out on shallow baking pan. Roast 50–60 minutes until nuts are fragrant and lightly browned. Low and slow is the key to successful roasting.

2: **PREPARE PRODUCE.** Wash and thoroughly dry the green leaf lettuce. Tear it into bite-sized pieces. Wash and dry the jicama, peel, and cut julienne (matchstick pieces). Wash and dry the clementines, peel by hand, and cut into thin, round slices. Set produce aside.

3: **PREPARE VINAIGRETTE.**

4: **ASSEMBLE SALAD.** Arrange lettuce leaves in a large shallow bowl or platter, and decorate with clementines. Sprinkle with cheese, pepitas, and fresh cilantro. Just before serving, drizzle with Cilantro Vinaigrette.

Cilantro Vinaigrette

¼ c. rice vinegar
2 tbsp. cilantro, minced
1 tbsp. sweet onion, chopped
2 tbsp. honey
1 tbsp. Dijon mustard
1 tsp. sea salt
1 tsp. ground black pepper
1 c. olive oil

Pour vinegar, cilantro, onion, honey, mustard, salt, and pepper into a small blender. Blend together until smooth, and pour into a quart-sized glass bowl. Slowly whisk or blend in the olive oil until emulsified. Set aside, and keep cool until ready to assemble salad.

Dried Fig and Cara Cara Orange Salad with Cara Cara Vinaigrette

THE SUPERB FLAVORS and textures of this salad—the Cara Cara oranges, the dried figs, and the Marcona almonds—will make this recipe a seasonal favorite.

20 dried figs

7 oz. baby spinach leaves

4 Cara Cara oranges

1 c. San Andreas cheese, (or other local Pecorino-style cheese) grated large

1 c. fair trade Marcona almonds (buy roasted and salted, if possible)

1: **PREPARE PRODUCE.** Snip off the hard stems of the dried figs, and then with a sharp paring knife, cut each fig in half from the top tip of the stem to the bottom of the fig. If your knife gets sticky, run in under hot water and continue cutting. Set aside until ready to assemble salads. Wash and thoroughly dry the spinach. Rinse the oranges, and with a sharp paring knife, peel away the skin from the fruit. Working over a bowl to reserve the juice, cut along both sides of each dividing membrane, and lift out sections from center. Set the orange segments aside. Measure out at least ¼ c. of reserved juice for the vinaigrette. Juice an extra orange if necessary.

2: **PREPARE VINAIGRETTE.**

3: **ASSEMBLE SALADS.** Divide spinach between 8 pretty bowls or salad plates, arrange orange segments on each salad, and sprinkle with grated cheese. Create a flower blossom on top with dried figs, and set Marcona almonds in the center of each blossom. Just before serving, drizzle with Cara Cara Vinaigrette.

Cara Cara Vinaigrette

¼ c. fresh-squeezed Cara Cara orange juice

2 tbsp. rice vinegar

2 tbsp. honey

½ tsp. Dijon mustard

¼ tsp. shallot, chopped

1 tsp. sea salt

½ tsp. black pepper

1 c. golden olive oil

Pour reserved Cara Cara orange juice, rice vinegar, honey, mustard, shallot, sea salt, and pepper into a small blender. Blend to combine, and pour into a glass bowl. Slowly whisk in the olive oil until emulsified. Pour into a glass jar, cover, and keep cool until ready to assemble.

Keep It Fresh

When purchasing the dried figs, look for the un-sulphured (may look darker and be a little drier but still have great flavor) and "low or no sugar added" brands when possible. Look for organic dried figs grown closest to your home; or buy fair trade. Store figs refrigerated in an airtight container to maintain freshness up to 1 year.

Winter Black Grape Salad with Sweet Balsamic Vinaigrette

CARR VALLEY Cheese Company, in Wisconsin, makes the Marisa Cheese featured in this salad. It is a cave-aged, sheep-milk cheese that was named after their master cheese maker's daughter. For more information on Carr Valley Cheese go to www.carrvalleycheese.com. The peppery mizuna greens, the sweet and juicy black grapes, the crunchy almonds, and the flavorful cheese in this recipe provide an amazing blend of tastes and textures.

4 c. seedless black grapes
7 oz. mixed mizuna greens (Asian greens)
½ c. roasted almonds (see recipe on page 13)
4 oz. aged Carr Valley Marisa Cheese, shaved
(or a comparable local cheese)

1: **PREPARE VINAIGRETTE.**

2: **PREPARE PRODUCE.** Wash the grapes. Set aside 32 of the grapes to garnish the salads. Slice the rest of the grapes in little rounds and set aside. Wash and thoroughly dry the mizuna greens. Trim off any long stems.

3: **ASSEMBLE SALADS.** Divide greens on 8 pretty salad plates, decorate with grape slices, and sprinkle with almonds. Shave 3 slices of cheese on each salad, arrange 4 whole grapes in the center of each salad, and, just before serving, drizzle with Sweet Balsamic Vinaigrette.

Sweet Balsamic Vinaigrette

6 tbsp. balsamic vinegar
2 tbsp. frozen grape juice concentrate
½ tsp. shallot, chopped
1 tsp. Inglehoffer Sweet Hot Mustard (or Dijon)
1 tsp. sea salt
1 tsp. ground black pepper
½ c. fruity green olive oil

Place balsamic vinegar, grape juice concentrate, shallot, mustard, salt, and pepper into a small blender. Blend to combine, and pour into a glass bowl. Slowly whisk in the olive oil until emulsified. Pour into a glass jar, cover, and keep cool until ready to assemble salad.

Irish Potato Cabbage Salad
with Green Parsley and Mustard Vinaigrette

MANY PEOPLE associate corned beef and cabbage with traditional St. Patrick's Day fare. This recipe pays homage to Irish history and brings an ancient recipe into the twenty-first century. Happy St. Patrick's Day!

3 lb. corned beef brisket
16–20 baby Yukon Gold potatoes
2 tbsp. green onion, chopped
¼ c. fresh parsley, chopped
2 c. red cabbage
2 c. green cabbage

1: **PREPARE CORNED BEEF.** Cook corned beef brisket according to package or market directions. Cut into bite-sized, matchstick pieces, and put into a 3-qt. glass bowl.

2: **PREPARE PRODUCE.** Wash and cut the baby Yukon Gold potatoes in halves. Boil until the potatoes are cooked through, drain, and put into the bowl with the cooked brisket. Wash, dry, and chop fine the green onions and parsley. Add to the 3-qt. bowl and toss together with brisket and potatoes. Wash, dry, and tear the cabbage into bite-sized shreds. Set aside.

3: **PREPARE VINAIGRETTE.**

4: **ASSEMBLE SALAD.** Add cabbage to warm potatoes, brisket, parsley, and onions, and fold in the Green Parsley and Mustard Vinaigrette. Serve at room temperature.

Green Parsley and Mustard Vinaigrette

6 tbsp. balsamic vinegar
½ tsp. shallot, chopped
2 tbsp. local honey
2 tsp.s stone-ground mustard
¼ c. fresh parsley, chopped

1 tsp. sea salt
1 tsp. ground black pepper
½ c. fruity green olive oil

Place balsamic vinegar, shallot, honey, mustard, parsley, salt, and pepper into a small blender. Blend to combine, and pour into a glass bowl. Slowly whisk in the olive oil until emulsified. Pour into a glass jar, cover, and keep cool until ready to assemble salad.

Corned Beef

The term "corned" beef comes from the processing of the meat used long ago when pellets of salt, the size of corn kernels, were rubbed into the beef to preserve it. Today, saltwater is used for brining instead. When purchasing your corned beef, check out your options: organic, grass-fed, or nitrite-free cured meat.

Winter Bitter Greens Salad with Sweet Apple and Cinnamon Vinaigrette

THE SLIGHTLY SWEET, mild Florence fennel, with its green, feathery foliage, adds great flavor and texture to this salad. Look for brightly colored stems and greens with a fragrant aroma.

7 oz. winter bitter greens (a combination of endive, arugula, mizuna, and escarole)

½ c. Florence fennel (bulb variety)

2 c. Grafton Village Cheese Company Classic Reserve Cheddar, grated (or use a comparable local cheddar cheese)

½ c. raw walnuts

1: **PREPARE PRODUCE.** Wash and thoroughly dry the bitter greens. Wash, dry, and trim the bulb of fennel. Slice off the stems and save if desired. Cut off the hard base of the bulb. Grate the fennel (large grate) and set aside.

2: **PREPARE VINAIGRETTE.**

3: **ASSEMBLE SALAD.** In a large, shallow bowl, arrange the mixed bitter greens, and gently toss with the grated cheese and fennel. Add raw walnuts, and just before serving, drizzle with Sweet Apple and Cinnamon Vinaigrette.

Sweet Apple and Cinnamon Vinaigrette

¼ c. rice vinegar

3 tbsp. frozen apple juice concentrate

1 tbsp. local honey

2 tbsp. red onion, minced

1 tbsp. Dijon mustard

¼ tsp. cinnamon

½ tsp. sea salt

½ tsp. ground black pepper

½ c. walnut oil

Place rice vinegar, apple juice concentrate, honey, onion, mustard, cinnamon, salt, and pepper into a small blender. Blend to combine, and pour into a glass bowl. Slowly whisk in the walnut oil until emulsified. Pour into a glass jar, cover, and keep cool until ready to assemble salad.

Winter Chopped Super Salad with Pomegranate Vinaigrette

POMEGRANATES, first grown in northern Iran or Turkey between 4000 B.C. and 3000 B.C., are believed to be the earliest cultivated fruit. This exquisite fruit makes this salad both visually appealing and a delight for your palate.

2 c. water

2 c. red quinoa

2 medium pomegranates (for 1 c. of seeds)

2 oz. spinach

2 oz. green kale

2 oz. baby bok choy

½ c. dried blueberries

½ c. dried cranberries

½ c. dried acai berries

2 c. red grapes

1½ c. tamari-roasted pumpkin seeds
(purchase this prepared)

2 tbsp. ground, roasted flaxseed
(purchase this prepared)

1: **PREPARE QUINOA.** Bring 2 c. water and red quinoa to a boil. Cover and turn down the heat to low. Simmer for 15 minutes and then lift up the cover and stir. Quinoa should be firm but cooked through. When it is done, the grain turns slightly transparent, and the curly, stringlike germ has separated from the circular part. Drain well, and set aside to cool.

2: **PREPARE POMEGRANATE** according to directions on page 133.

3: **PREPARE OTHER PRODUCE.** Wash, thoroughly dry, and cut chiffonade into bite-sized pieces the spinach, kale (remove from center rib), and baby bok choy.

4: **PREPARE VINAIGRETTE.**

5: **ASSEMBLE SALAD.** Place all of the salad ingredients into a large 3-qt. glass mixing bowl. Drizzle with Pomegranate Vinaigrette, and serve immediately.

Pomegranate Vinaigrette

1 medium pomegranate
¼ c. balsamic vinegar
2 tbsp. local honey
1 tsp. Dijon mustard
1 tsp. sea salt
½ tsp. ground black pepper
½ c. pumpkin seed oil or olive oil

Cut 1 pomegranate in half, and juice on an orange juicer, removing ⅛ c. of juice. Place balsamic vinegar, pomegranate juice, honey, mustard, salt, and pepper into a small blender and blend. Pour into a glass bowl. Slowly whisk in the pumpkin seed oil (or olive oil) until emulsified. Pour into a glass jar, cover, and keep cool until ready to assemble salad.

Tamari Tofu Cobb Salad
with Simple Winter Vinaigrette

TOFU SEASONED with tamari, a naturally brewed soy sauce with a smooth, complex flavor, adds depth to this recipe. Look for tamari that is labeled "non-GMO" or organic.

1 lb. tofu

1 c. tamari (a variety of soy sauce)

2 c. frozen early green peas

2 c. frozen edamame

7 oz. green leaf lettuce

3 c. whole baby carrots

4 cooked and sliced golden beets

4 red beets, cooked and julienne cut

1½ c. roasted sunflower seeds
   (see recipe on page 13)

1 c. sprigs fresh herbs for garnish

1: **PREPARE VINAIGRETTE** by following recipe on page 128.

2: **PREPARE TOFU.** Put the tofu into a small glass loaf pan, and pour the vinaigrette tamari mixture over the tofu. Refrigerate for 1–2 hours.

   Preheat oven to 350°F, and bake for 50–60 minutes. Let cool and then cut into julienne pieces.

3: **PREPARE PRODUCE.** Thaw and drain the peas and the edamame. Set aside. Wash and thoroughly dry the green leaf lettuce. Tear into medium-sized pieces. Wash and dry carrots. Cut in halves the long way. Wash and dry beets. Peel and cut julienne or slice into rounds.

4: **ASSEMBLE SALADS.** Arrange greens on 8 pretty salad plates. On each salad, make little rows of the tofu, carrots, beets, peas, and edamame. Sprinkle with sunflower seeds, garnish with a sprig of fresh herbs, and, just before serving, drizzle with Simple Winter Vinaigrette.

Tofu

Tofu, a soybean product, is a great source of protein. It is not very flavorful on its own but takes on the flavors of marinades and foods with which it is cooked. Tofu, also known as soybean curd or bean curd, is creamy and smooth but firm enough to slice. It is quite perishable and should be kept refrigerated and used within a week. If it's packaged in water, the water should be drained and changed daily. Since many soybeans are genetically modified in the U.S., look for tofu and tamari that are labeled "non-GMO" or organic. Organic products are not allowed to contain any GMOs (genetically modified organisms). For more information, go to www.organicconsumers.org.

Winter Green Salad
with Green Apple and Basil Vinaigrette

HAZELNUTS, also called filberts or cobnuts, add a nice crunch and flavor to this recipe, while wedges of Rogue Creamery Echo Mountain Blue Cheese contribute a welcome creaminess. The Rogue Creamery is an artisan cheese company dedicated to sustainability and the art and tradition of making cheese by hand. If the Echo Mountain Blue is not available, ask your cheese monger for a comparable local substitute.

7 oz. baby spinach

4 large Granny Smith apples (or other green apple variety)

2 c. seedless green grapes

4 oz. Rogue Creamery Echo Mountain Blue Cheese, cut in wedges (or a comparable local blue cheese)

½ c. roasted hazelnuts (see recipe on page 13)

8 pretty sprigs of fresh basil

1: **PREPARE VINAIGRETTE.**

2: **PREPARE PRODUCE.** Wash and dry spinach, and set aside. Wash and dry apples and grapes. Cut apples into thin slices (see photo).

3: **ASSEMBLE SALADS.** Arrange greens on 8 salad plates. Fan apple slices in a circle on the greens. Tuck in 2–3 wedges of cheese between apples, sprinkle with whole-roasted hazelnuts, and garnish each with grapes and a sprig of basil. Just before serving, drizzle with Green Apple and Basil Vinaigrette.

Green Apple and Basil Vinaigrette

¼ c. white champagne vinegar

2 tbsp. frozen apple juice concentrate

4 tbsp. minced basil

1 tbsp. sweet Vidalia or Walla Walla onion

1 tsp. sea salt

1 tsp. ground black pepper

1 tsp. champagne-style mustard (such as SoNo Trading Company Champagne Garlic mustard)

½ c. really special green and fruity rich olive oil

Put the champagne vinegar, apple juice concentrate, basil, onion, sea salt, pepper, and mustard into a small blender. Blend together until smooth, and pour into a quart-sized glass bowl. Slowly whisk in the olive oil until emulsified. Set aside in cool place until ready to serve.

Chipotle Caesar Salad
with Creamy Chipotle Caesar Dressing

SERVES 6–8

THOUGHT TO HAVE been created by Italian chef Caesar Cardini in 1924, traditional Caesar salads consist of romaine lettuce, grated parmesan, croutons, egg, and sometimes anchovies tossed with garlic vinaigrette dressing. With chipotle and chili in the dressing and avocado and tortilla chip croutons in the salad, this recipe puts a delicious Southwest twist on the classic Caesar.

16 black corn tortilla chips
½ c. SarVecchio Asiago cheese, medium grated
7 oz. romaine lettuce
16 sweet grape tomatoes
4 ripe avocados

1: **PREPARE TORTILLA CROUTONS.** Preheat oven to 270°F. Spread out tortilla chips on cookie sheet, sprinkle with ¼ c. finely grated cheese, and bake until cheese is melted and golden. Remove from oven and cool.

2: **PREPARE DRESSING.**

3: **PREPARE PRODUCE.** Wash and thoroughly dry the romaine. Tear into bite-sized pieces. Wash and dry the grape tomatoes. Cut into halves. Wash and dry the avocados. Score avocado skin along the north–south axis. Gently twist halves apart, and score the halves again north–south. Slice into quarters, pull from pit, peel skin away, and remove the pit. Cut each quarter in half and then into bite-sized chunks.

4: **ASSEMBLE SALAD.** Just before serving, place romaine, tomatoes, cheese, and Creamy Chipotle Caesar Dressing into a large mixing bowl. Gently toss together. This can be plated immediately and served with a couple of the tortilla croutons on top, or you can serve this salad right from the bowl and put the tortilla chips in a pretty basket on the side.

Creamy Chipotle Caesar Dressing

6 tbsp. lime juice
2 tbsp. honey
1 tbsp. fresh cilantro
1/16 tsp. chipotle chili powder
½ clove garlic (more if you love garlic)
1 tsp. sea salt
1 tsp. ground black pepper
1½ c. olive oil–based mayonnaise
2 tbsp. extra-virgin olive oil
½ c. SarVecchio Asiago cheese, finely grated (or comparable local asiago cheese)

Put lime juice, honey, fresh cilantro, chipotle chili powder, garlic, sea salt, and black pepper into a small blender. Blend together until smooth, and pour into a glass bowl. Slowly fold in the mayonnaise, olive oil, and finely grated cheese. Blend all together, pour into a small glass jar, and set aside in a cool place until ready to use.

Garbanzo and Greens Salad with Lemon Tahini Dressing

SERVES 6–8

THIS MIDDLE EASTERN inspired salad features the mild, slightly nutty flavor of garbanzo beans and the tangy tastes of lemon and tahini. Garbanzo beans, also called chickpeas, are a good source of protein and are available fresh, dried, or canned.

15-oz. can cooked garbanzo beans (or comparable measure of dried beans cooked)

1 tbsp. olive oil

⅛ tsp. cumin powder

⅛ tsp. cinnamon

⅛ tsp. allspice

¼ tsp. sea salt

7 oz. mixed baby greens

1 sweet red bell pepper

1 sweet yellow bell pepper

1 c. Chase Hill Farm Feta cheese, crumbled

1: **PREPARE GARBANZO BEANS.** Preheat oven to 350°F. Drain garbanzo beans into a colander, and rinse well with cold water until no more foam appears. Let beans drain, and pat dry thoroughly. Toss with olive oil, cumin, cinnamon, allspice, and sea salt. Arrange in a single layer on baking sheet, and roast 40–50 minutes or until they are slightly browned and make a rattling sound when you shake the baking sheet. Set aside to cool. They will be a crunchy and crispy treat.

2: **PREPARE DRESSING.**

3: **PREPARE PRODUCE.** Wash and thoroughly dry the greens. Wash, dry, and cut stems off peppers. Cut in half, and remove the seeds and white membranes from the inside of the peppers. Cut julienne style in 1½-in. matchstick pieces.

4: **ASSEMBLE SALAD.** This salad can be served plated or on a platter with serving tongs. Arrange greens on plates or on large salad platter. Decorate with red and yellow peppers, sprinkle with feta cheese and garbanzos, and serve the Lemon Tahini Dressing on the side in a pretty serving pitcher with a spoon.

Lemon Tahini Dressing

¼ c. lemon juice

1 tbsp. honey

1 tbsp. tamari

2 tbsp. sesame tahini

2 tbsp. sweet onion

2 tbsp. chopped fresh parsley

½ tsp. sea salt

½ tsp. ground black pepper

½ c. olive oil

¼ c. Greek-style yogurt

Pour lemon juice, honey, tamari, sesame tahini, onion, parsley, sea salt, and ground pepper into blender. Blend together until smooth, pour into bowl, and slowly whisk in olive oil and yogurt. Blend until smooth and creamy. Set aside until ready to dress salad.

Citron-Roasted Brussels Sprout Salad with Fresh Rosemary and Meyer Lemon Vinaigrette

THIS BRIGHTLY FLAVORED, unique salad is tossed in a lemony vinaigrette made with Meyer lemons. Originally from China, Meyer lemons were introduced in the United States in 1908. A cross between a lemon and a mandarin orange, Meyers are sweeter, juicier, and rounder than conventional lemons.

2 lb. brussels sprouts

3 tbsp. olive oil

½ tsp. sea salt

½ tsp. fine-ground black pepper

2 tbsp. lemon zest

1 c. roasted pine nuts (see recipe on page 13)

½ c. SarVecchio Parmesan cheese, grated

Fresh Rosemary and Meyer Lemon Vinaigrette

¼ c. fresh Meyer lemon juice
1 tsp. Dijon mustard
2 tbsp. local honey
1 tsp. fresh rosemary

1 tsp. sea salt
½ tsp. ground black pepper
½ c. olive oil

Put lemon juice, mustard, honey, fresh rosemary, salt, and ground pepper into a small kitchen blender. Blend to combine, and pour into a glass bowl. Slowly whisk in the olive oil until emulsified, and keep cool until ready to assemble salad.

1: **PREPARE BRUSSELS SPROUTS.** Increase oven heat to 400°F. Cut off the brown ends of the brussels sprouts, and pull off any yellow outer leaves. Cut in halves. Put brussels sprouts into a large mixing bowl, and toss with olive oil, sea salt, pepper, and lemon zest to combine. Spread brussels sprouts out on a cookie sheet, and roast for 25–30 minutes, until browned and crisp on the outside. Remove from oven, and set aside to cool.

2: **PREPARE VINAIGRETTE.**

3: **ASSEMBLE SALAD.** Place all salad ingredients in a large glass serving bowl. Gently toss together with Fresh Rosemary and Meyer Lemon Vinaigrette, and sprinkle with roasted pine nuts and cheese. Keep cool until ready to serve.

Pink Pummelo and Heart of Palm Salad with Honey Pepper Vinaigrette

THIS RECIPE features two unique varieties of produce: pink pummelo and hearts of palm. Pummelo, or pomelo, is the largest of all citrus fruits, ranging in size from a baby cantaloupe to almost basketball size! This massive fruit has a mild, sweet grapefruit flavor and is a good source of vitamin A, vitamin C, calcium, and potassium. Hearts of palm, the edible inner portion of the stem of the cabbage palm tree, are ivory-hued, thin spears with a delicate flavor akin to that of an artichoke.

7 oz. fresh watercress

4–6 ripe pummelos (grapefruit size)

14-oz. can hearts of palm

1½ c. roasted cashews (see recipe on page 13)

Cracked pepper

8 small sprigs or leaves of watercress (for garnish)

1 tsp. curly zests of pummelo (for garnish)

1: **PREPARE VINAIGRETTE.**

2: **PREPARE PRODUCE.** Wash, trim off any long stems, and thoroughly dry the watercress. Wash and dry the pummelos. With a sharp paring knife, peel away the thick skin and pith from the fruit. Working over a bowl to reserve the juice, cut along both sides of each dividing membrane, and lift out sections from center. Discard the seeds and pith. Save the skin if desired. Cut the fruit segments into bite-sized chunks, and set into a strainer over the bowl to keep collecting juices. Drain, rinse, and pat dry the hearts of palm. Slice the segments into uniform rounds and then in half moons.

3: **ASSEMBLE SALAD.** Divide watercress among 8 pretty salad plates. Arrange pummelo sections alternately with the hearts of palm in a blossom on the watercress, sprinkle with whole cashews, a crack of pepper, and a sprig of watercress. Just before serving, drizzle with Honey Pepper Vinaigrette. Add curly zests of pumello for garnish.

Honey Pepper Vinaigrette

¼ c. rice vinegar

2 tbsp. pummelo juice

4 tbsp. local honey

2 tbsp. Vidalia or Walla Walla onion, minced

1 tsp. sea salt

½ tsp. pink peppercorns

½ c. golden buttery olive oil

Put vinegar, pumello juice, honey, onion, sea salt, and pink peppercorns into a small blender. Blend ingredients together until well combined and smooth, and pour into a glass bowl. Slowly whisk in the olive oil until it is combined and emulsified. Pour into a glass jar, and set aside in a cool place until ready to use.

Tarragon Chicken and Napa Cabbage Salad with Creamy Tarragon Dressing

NAPA CABBAGE, also known as Peking cabbage, is often confused with bok choy and Chinese cabbage, but Napa is a very different variety. It is superior in flavor and contains more calcium and vitamin A than regular cabbage. This salad is wonderful for a light lunch or a prelude to dinner. If you're lucky enough to have leftovers, wrap it in a tortilla for a meal the next day.

7 oz. Napa cabbage

1 red Anjou pear

1 yellow Anjou pear

2 c. seedless green grapes

1 c. fresh tarragon

3 c. cooked chicken breast, cubed

½ c. dried dates, chopped

½ c. cooked crisp diagonally snipped hickory-smoked bacon

1½ c. roasted pecans (see recipe on page 13)

1: **PREPARE PRODUCE.** Wash and thoroughly dry Napa cabbage. Cut chiffonade style into bite-sized pieces. Wash and dry pears and grapes. Slice pears and cut into small pieces. Cut grapes in halves. Rinse tarragon and pat dry. Remove leaves from stems, and chop fine. Reserve sprigs for garnish.

2: **PREPARE DRESSING.**

3: **SALAD ASSEMBLY.** Put all salad ingredients (except for the Napa cabbage) into a large, 3-qt. mixing bowl. Fold in half of the Creamy Tarragon Dressing, and combine well. Put remaining dressing into a little serving pitcher with a spoon for cabbage. Refrigerate until ready to serve. Just before serving, add the pecans. On 8 pretty dinner or salad plates, create a little nest of Napa cabbage, and scoop approximately ½ c. of Tarragon Chicken Salad on each bed of cabbage. Garnish with a sprig of tarragon, and serve with the reserved Creamy Tarragon Dressing.

Creamy Tarragon Dressing

½ c. fresh lemon juice

2 tbsp. sweet Vidalia onion, chopped

4 tbsp. fresh tarragon

4 tbsp. honey

2 tsp. sea salt

1 tsp. ground black pepper

½ c. Greek-style plain yogurt

½ c. fresh heavy cream

1 c. olive oil–based mayonnaise

Put lemon juice, onion, tarragon, honey, sea salt, and pepper into a blender. Blend until combined and smooth. Pour into a 2-qt. glass bowl, and gently whisk in the yogurt, cream, and mayonnaise until well combined. Keep cool until salad assembly.

Resources

CHEESE AND CHOCOLATE

ALEMAR CHEESE COMPANY
www.alemarcheese.com
Bent River Camembert is made by the Alemar Cheese Company in Minnesota.

BELLWETHER FARMS
www.bellwetherfarms.com
Bellwether Farms, a farmstead cheese maker in California, makes a cheese named San Andreas. It is a full-flavored, smooth, pecorino-style cheese and is made from raw sheep milk.

CARR VALLEY CHEESE
www.carrvalleycheese.com
Family owned and located in Wisconsin, Carr Valley Cheese has produced cheese for more than a hundred years.

CHASE HILL FARM
www.chasehillfarm.com
Chase Hill Farm, located in Massachusetts, is a family-owned, organic-certified dairy farm that makes wonderful, sustainable cheese.

CRAVE BROTHERS
www.cravecheese.com
The Crave Brothers Farmstead in Wisconsin creates award-winning, fresh mozzarellas.

DAGOBA ORGANIC CHOCOLATE
www.dagobachocolate.com
Dagoba Organic Chocolate is a company based in Oregon that works diligently to produce organic, sustainably grown chocolate products.

FARIBAULT DAIRY
www.faribaultdairy.com
The Faribault Dairy in Minnesota (recently purchased by Swiss Valley Farms Cooperative of Iowa, www.swissvalley.com) makes Amablu Gorgonzola Cheese and St. Pete's Select Blue Cheese.

GRAFTON VILLAGE CHEESE COMPANY
www.graftonvillagecheese.com
The Grafton Village Cheese Company in Vermont makes amazing aged cheddar cheeses that are handcrafted from the milk of local family farms. Grafton Village cheddar has no chemical additives, synthetic growth hormones, or preservatives.

HIDDEN SPRINGS CREAMERY
www.hiddenspringscreamery.com
Hidden Springs Creamery, located in Wisconsin, produces a wonderful sheep's milk feta cheese.

MILTON CREAMERY
www.miltoncreamery.com
The Milton Creamery, a family-owned company in Iowa, makes a delicious cheese called Prairie Breeze.

MOZZARELLA COMPANY
www.mozzco.com
The Mozzarella Company, based in Texas, makes all of its cheese, including its Queso Oaxaca Mexican Mozzarella, by hand following centuries-old recipes.

ORGANIC VALLEY
www.organicvalley.coop
With farms across the country, Organic Valley's mission is to save family farms through organic agriculture. It produces a variety of organic dairy products, including many delicious cheeses.

PASTURELAND DAIRY COOPERATIVE
www.pastureland.coop
Based in Minnesota, PastureLand Dairy Cooperative produces organic cheeses, including Farmdog Blue and Goodhue Grass-fed Gouda Cheese.

ROGUE CREAMERY
www.roguecreamery.com
The Rogue Creamery in Oregon produced the first smoked blue cheese, named Oregon Blue. The creamery now produces a number of other blue cheeses, including its Echo Mountain Blue.

ROTH KÄSE
www.rothkase.com
Roth Käse, an award-winning cheese maker in Wisconsin, produces Solé GranQueso, which has been compared to the famous Spanish Manchego.

SARTORI FOODS
www.sartorifoods.com
Sartori Foods produces the award-winning SarVecchio Parmesan and SarVecchio Asiago cheeses.

STICKNEY HILL DAIRY
www.stickneydairy.com
Using no antibiotics or hormones, the Stickney Hill Dairy Farms in Minnesota makes a delicious goat's milk chèvre.

UPLANDS CHEESE COMPANY
www.uplandscheese.com
Uplands Cheese Company (owned by two neighboring families in Wisconsin) makes a very unique farmstead cheese called Pleasant Ridge Reserve Cheese.

GREEN RESOURCES

THE DAILY GREEN
www.thedailygreen.com
This is a great website with guides for Green Living, Green Cuisine, Living Green, and the latest news and research.

DISCOVERY CHANNEL'S PLANET GREEN
www.planetgreen.discovery.com
Hosted by the Discovery Channel, this website has a wealth of "green" information in the following categories: Food & Health, Home & Garden, Tech & Transport, Fashion & Beauty, Travel & Outdoors, and Work & Connect.

EAT WELL GUIDE
www.eatwellguide.org
Eat Well Guide is a free online directory of fresh, locally grown, and sustainably produced food in the United States and Canada. The listings include family farms, restaurants, farmers' markets, grocery stores, community supported agriculture (CSA) programs, pick-your-own orchards, and more.

ENVIRONMENTAL WORKING GROUP
www.ewg.org/safefishlist
The Environmental Working Group provides information regarding the safety of seafood. The website also provides research on the pesticide loads of conventionally grown produce, the safest sunscreens to use, and cell phone radiation statistics. The group also produces the website www.foodnews.org, which provides research and information on the pesticide loads of conventionally grown produce.

GREENER CHOICES
www.greenerchoices.org
Launched on Earth Day 2005 by Consumers Union, the nonprofit publisher of *Consumer Reports*, this web-based initiative informs consumers about environmentally friendly products and practices.

INSTITUTE FOR RESPONSIBLE TECHNOLOGY
www.nongmoshoppingguide.com
The Institute for Responsible Technology, a leader in educating policymakers and the public about genetically modified (GM) foods and crops, hosts this website.

LOCAL HARVEST
www.localharvest.org
This website is an excellent tool for locating farmers' markets, restaurants, family farms, community assisted agriculture (CSA) programs, and other sources of sustainably grown food in your area.

MARINE STEWARDSHIP COUNCIL
www.msc.org
This is the website of the Marine Stewardship Council (MSC). You will find extensive information on the sustainability standards MSC requires, and you can use the search tool to find MSC-certified seafood in your area.

MONTEREY BAY AQUARIUM
www.mbayaq.org
This is the website of the Monterey Bay Aquarium, which has a very thorough list of sustainable and healthy seafood. Go to the "Save the Oceans" heading, "Seafood Watch," and "Seafood Recommendations." An iPhone app is also available.

ORGANIC CONSUMERS ASSOCIATION
www.organicconsumers.org
This website of the Organic Consumers Association provides information on organic standards; news on health issues, food safety, and genetic engineering; and an extensive "green" business directory.

ORGANIC PRAIRIE
www.organicprairie.coop
Organic Prairie sells healthful, wholesome, and humanely raised meats. The company's website has great information about the benefits of selecting organic meats under the "Why Choose OP" (Organic Prairie) heading.

PESTICIDE ACTION NETWORK'S WHAT'S ON MY FOOD
www.whatsonmyfood.com
This is a website of the Pesticide Action Network, providing extensive information on the pesticides found on produce and some other foods, including meats, grains, honey, and milk.

PICK-YOUR-OWN FARMS
www.pickyourown.org
This website is a wonderful tool to find a pick-your-own farm near you—apples, strawberries, pumpkins, cherries, and much, much more. Information is also provided on how to can and freeze your produce and how to make jams and jellies.

STAR PRAIRIE TROUT FARM
www.starprairietrout.com
Star Prairie Trout Farm, in Wisconsin, raises trout on pure feed without additives or medication in pristine, 100 percent spring water. Trout is sold commercially, or you can fish on-site and catch your own.

First published in 2011 by Voyageur Press, an imprint of MBI Publishing Company, 400 First Avenue North, Suite 300, Minneapolis, MN 55401 USA

Copyright © 2011 by Pam Powell
Photography © Paul Markert Photography
Illustrations © Pam Powell

The information in this book is true and complete to the best of our knowledge. All recommendations are made without any guarantee on the part of the author or Publisher, who also disclaims any liability incurred in connection with the use of this data or specific details.

We recognize, further, that some words, model names, and designations mentioned herein are the property of the trademark holder. We use them for identification purposes only. This is not an official publication.

Voyageur Press titles are also available at discounts in bulk quantity for industrial or sales-promotional use. For details write to Special Sales Manager at MBI Publishing Company, 400 First Avenue North, Suite 300, Minneapolis, MN 55401 USA.

To find out more about our books, visit us online at www.voyageurpress.com.

ISBN-13: 978-0-7603-4043-1

Library of Congress Cataloging-in-Publication Data

Powell, Pam, 1956-
 Salad days : recipes for delicious organic salads and dressings for every season / Pam Powell ; photographs by Paul Markert.
   p. cm.
 Includes index.
 ISBN 978-0-7603-4043-1 (flexibound)
 1. Salads. 2. Salad dressing. 3. Natural foods. 4. Cookbooks. I. Title.
TX807.P68 2011
641.8'3--dc22

                         2010045484

Editor: Kari Cornell
Design Manager: Katie Sonmor
Designed by Sandra Salamony
Illustrations by Pam Powell

Index

Acknowledgments

I HAVE BEEN SO FORTUNATE to be blessed with a close, supportive group of family and friends who share my enthusiasm and joy in the preparation of fresh organic foods. I am especially grateful to my best friend, taste tester, and supportive husband of twenty-four years, Jim Powell, and my son Nick and his wife Anna. It is truly because of their unconditional love and support, steadfast hard work, creative expertise, and total commitment that we were able to create the Salad Girl Organic Salad Dressing Company, which allowed me the opportunity to write this darling salad book and share all of my favorite salad recipes.

Throughout this book you will find tips on how to be "greener" with your salads. These tips were authored by the talented writer, Sarah Baron Sullivan. Sarah writes quarterly e-letters to market my Salad Girl Organic Dressings. She also writes for and edits my Salad Girl blog, www.thesaladgirlsblog.com.

My thanks to photographer Paul Markert for creating these beautiful images and bringing my salads to life!

Many thanks to Jean Walberg , Roddie Turner, Bill Harmon, Jennifer Harmon, and Jean Schissel for offering their lovely dishes and beautiful homes to us for our chapter photo shoots. I am so grateful.

To my sweet sister Patti and to my wonderful brothers David, Steve, and Kevin. Thank you for having faith in me and for all of your loving support.

My dear friend, designer and stylist for HDI.Studios.com, Jennifer Harmon: thank you for all of your hard work and creativity and guidance to style each salad and to create all the beautiful settings for each chapter.

To all the food writers and media folks who have taken time out of their busy schedules to chat up so kindly the Salad Girl company, including Kathy Jenkins, Rick Nelson, Stephanie Hanson, and Stephanie March.

And last but not least, thanks to Shari and Roger Wilsey for their generous introduction to Mary and Jim Kowalski who provided me with the opportunity to bring my organic salad dressings to the retail marketplace and for their continued support.